DEAD AND BURIED IN NEW ENGLAND

Respectful Visits to the Tombstones and Monuments of 306 Noteworthy Yankees

BY MARY MAYNARD

To Jim

YANKEE is a registered trademark of Yankee Publishing, Inc. Used by permission.

Printed in the United States of America on acid-free ∞ paper

Editors: Charles Gerras
         Anne Imhoff
Cover Designer: Stan Green
Cover Photographer: Susan Lapides
Interior Designer: Sandy Freeman

Library of Congress Cataloging-in-Publication Data

Maynard, Mary, 1929-
    Dead and buried in New England : respectful visits to the tombstones and monuments of 306 noteworthy Yankees / by Mary Maynard
        p.   cm.
    Includes index.
    ISBN 0-89909-363-9 paperback
    1. Tombs—New England—Guidebooks.   2. Celebrities—New England--Tombs—Guidebooks.   3. Cemeteries—New England—Guidebooks.   4. Sepulchral monuments—New England—Guidebooks.   5. New England--Biography.   I. Title.
F5.M388   1993
917.404′43—dc20   92–24810
                                                            CIP

Distributed in the book trade by St. Martin's Press

2   4   6   8   10   9   7   5   3   1   paperback

CONTENTS

CONNECTICUT

MAINE

NEW HAMPSHIRE

VERMONT

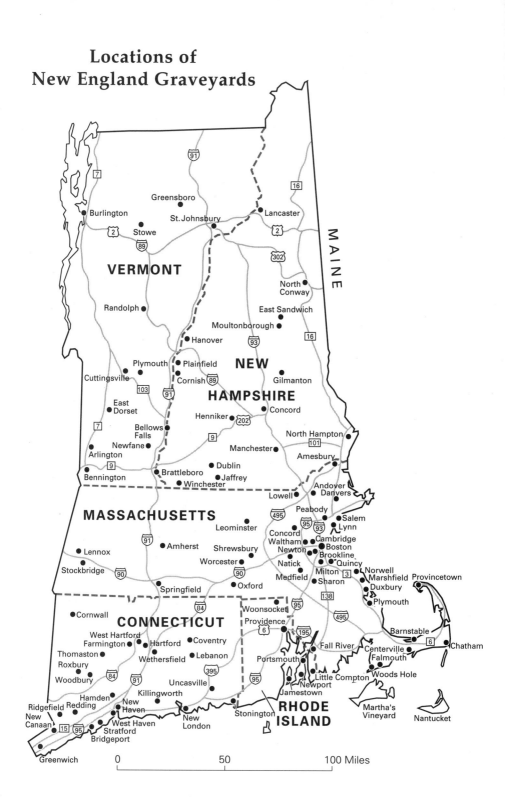

Locations of
New England Graveyards

VERMONT

Burlington
Greensboro
St. Johnsbury
Lancaster
Stowe
North Conway
Randolph
East Sandwich
Moultonborough
Hanover
Plymouth Plainfield
Cuttingsville
Cornish
Gilmanton
East Dorset
Concord
Henniker
Bellows Falls
North Hampton
Newfane
Manchester
Arlington
Amesbury
Dublin
Bennington Brattleboro Jaffrey
Winchester
Andover
Danvers
Lowell
Peabody
MASSACHUSETTS
Leominster
Salem
Concord
Lynn
Lennox
Waltham
Cambridge
Amherst Shrewsbury
Newton Boston
Stockbridge
Worcester
Brookline
Natick
Quincy
Springfield
Medfield
Milton
Norwell
Oxford
Sharon
Marshfield Provincetown
Duxbury
Plymouth
Cornwall
Woonsocket
CONNECTICUT
Providence
Barnstable
West Hartford
Farmington Hartford Coventry
Fall River
Centerville Chatham
Thomaston
Wethersfield Lebanon
Portsmouth
Falmouth
Roxbury
Woods Hole
Woodbury
Uncasville
Little Compton
Hamden
Killingworth
Newport
New Haven
Jamestown
Ridgefield Redding
New Canaan
West Haven
Stratford
New London
Stonington
RHODE ISLAND
Martha's Vineyard
Nantucket
Bridgeport
Greenwich

MAINE

NEW HAMPSHIRE

0   50   100 Miles

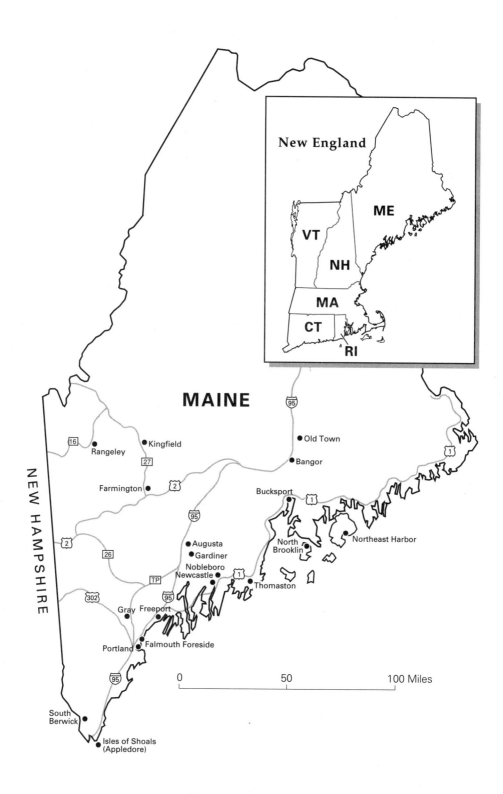

New England

ME

VT

NH

MA

CT

RI

MAINE

NEW HAMPSHIRE

95

16 ● Kingfield
Rangeley

27

● Old Town

● Bangor

1

Farmington ●

2

Bucksport ●

95

2

26

TP

302

● Augusta
● Gardiner

Nobleboro ●
Newcastle ●

1

North
Brooklin ●

● Northeast Harbor

● Thomaston

1

Gray ● Freeport ●

95

Portland ● Falmouth Foreside

95

South
Berwick ●

● Isles of Shoals
(Appledore)

0   50   100 Miles

FOREWORD

Visiting the grave sites of notable New Englanders has long been a favorite pastime for natives as well as tourists. On Boston's famous Freedom Trail—one of the most popular tourist attractions in New England—there are several stops along the way at old cemeteries. Here you will find many well-worn paths to the grave sites of Founding Fathers and Mothers, great statesmen and patriots as well as those of "Mother Goose" and "Hester Prynne" (heroine of Hawthorne's *The Scarlet Letter*).

In Concord, Massachusetts, the tour buses stop at Sleepy Hollow Cemetery almost as often as they do at the Old North Bridge. Even on cold, wintry days, people climb the rough steps to "Author's Ridge" to lay boughs of pine or spruce greens on the small tombstone of Louisa May Alcott or that of Henry David Thoreau.

On a recent summer day, students from as far away as Wisconsin had traveled to Lowell, Massachusetts, to take grave rubbings of Jack Kerouac's gravestone. And on Martha's Vineyard, admirers decorate John Belushi's and Lillian Hellman's tombstones with small pebbles and seashells carried up from the beach.

If you visit the small hillside cemetery in East Dorset, Vermont, where Bill Wilson, co-founder of Alcoholics Anonymous, is buried, you will not be alone, particularly in the summertime. Hundreds of thankful recovered alcoholics make a pilgrimage to this site each year, often leaving AA tokens atop his tombstone.

Grave sites of sports figures, politicians, artists, musicians and media personalities all have their share of devotees. Not all of their names are well known. For example, you probably never heard of Effie Canning Carlton, but if you visit her burial place in Waltham, Massachusetts, her small, flower-bedecked, highly polished granite stone will inform you that she composed "Rock-a-Bye Baby." Or just a few miles away, in Newton, a large oblong box tomb, that of Samuel F. Smith, another composer, proudly proclaims his contribution: "My Country 'Tis of Thee."

Some of those mentioned in this book were not New Englanders by birth but rather by choice—or at least opted to be buried here for one reason of another. Willa Cather, who was born in the Back Creek Valley of Virginia, was brought up in Red Cloud, Nebraska, and wrote such insightful stories about the early pioneer settlers of the west, was buried in a classic New England setting: a small churchyard cemetery, behind an old 18th-century meetinghouse in the little village of Jaffrey, New Hampshire.

More recently, during the latter part of the 20th century two particularly poignant memorials are continually sought out by visitors to New England: those of Christa McAuliffe, "Teacher in Space," in Concord, New Hampshire, and Samantha Smith, "America's Littlest Ambassador," in Augusta, Maine. Samantha is not actually buried here, but a beautiful life-size bronze statue has been erected in her honor on the state capitol grounds. Children and grown-ups alike continually bring fresh flowers to decorate these sites.

New England has had its share of questionable characters such as Lizzy Borden, Sacco and Vanzetti, and "The Boston Strangler" as well as curious characters such as P. T. Barnum; Joseph Palmer, who was "persecuted for wearing a beard;" and "Ocean Born Mary." This guide is filled with anecdotal stories of these and many other fascinating characters who are *Dead and Buried in New England.*

MASSACHUSETTS

The gravestone of New England's legendary Mother Goose,
Granary Burying Ground, Boston.

Greater Boston Area

In 17th-century rural New England, the custom of burying family members in a corner of the farmyard was a perfectly acceptable practice. Many of these old family burying plots can still be seen today as you travel along the backcountry roads of the northeastern states. The solemn gray slate markers, huddled haphazardly together and poking their narrow square or rounded tops above tall weeds, lean precariously toward each other. Most of the stones are so weathered with age that the inscriptions, once so carefully hand chiseled on their surface, are now barely legible.

In the more populated villages, a section of the churchyard was usually set aside for burials. As the town grew in size and population, community burial places were eventually established. King's Chapel Burying Ground, the oldest cemetery in Boston, is the best example of the early evolution of burial practices in Old New England.

Boston

There is probably no better place to start a book on notable grave sites in New England than Boston. Some of the oldest and most interesting cemeteries in the United States are here, and at least four of them are on the famous Freedom Trail, Boston's most celebrated tourist attraction.

The names on the old tombstones in the burying grounds of King's Chapel, Granary, Common and Copp's Hill read like a veritable who's who of American history. There are so many, in fact, that for the sake of brevity, only some of the most recognizable names are included here. Some of the old illegible stones have been replaced, and all of them have been rearranged, so as you stroll through these fascinating graveyards, please bear in mind the admonishment of renowned Chief Justice Oliver Wendell Holmes in describing King's Chapel Burying Ground: "The upright stones have been shuffled about like chessmen and nothing short of the Day of Judgment will tell whose death lies beneath. . . . Shame! Shame! Shame!"

King's Chapel Burying Ground
58 Tremont Street

Isaac Johnson, one of the first settlers and a leader of the Massachusetts Bay Company, built himself a small house on land that was given to him on the corner of what is now Tremont and School streets. He spent many happy hours toiling in his garden, and just before he died in 1630 he requested to be buried there. And so he was, in the southwest corner of his garden.

Death came quickly to many of the early colonists, and as no other burial place had been established, Isaac's garden soon became the community graveyard. An old Boston record notes, "Brother Johnson's garden is getting to be a poor place for vegetables."

For the next 30 years, as the little village of Boston prospered and grew, this small plot of land was to become the final resting place for the first generation of English settlers in America. The town's leading citizens of the day as well as some of the most humble were buried here.

In 1688, however, when the new royal governor, Sir Andros, arrived in town, he enraged the citizens by confiscating part of the old burial ground to build an Episcopal church—the Church of England (hence the name "King's Chapel"). From then on, the burial plot became a church graveyard where the bodies of the royal governors and British soldiers were laid to rest side by side with those of the Puritans.

Today, thousands of people visit this cemetery each year to walk among the weathered gravestones and to read the ancient inscriptions. Among the notables buried here are John Winthrop (1588–1649), the first governor of Massachusetts Bay Colony; Mary Chilton (d.1679), who claimed to be the first Pilgrim to have stepped foot on Plymouth Rock; her husband, John Winslow, whose stone is inscribed "Passenger on the *Mayflower*"; William Dawes, who made a midnight ride similar to that of Paul Revere; John Alden, son of Pilgrims John and Priscilla; two royal governors; several Puritan ministers and Elizabeth Pain. The latter was a young Puritan woman who was made to wear a bright red letter A on the bodice of her dress. Elizabeth and her minister had fallen in love and she bore him a child-out of wedlock. Two hundred years after her death, Nathaniel Hawthorne retold her story, that of Hester Prynne, in the classic novel *The Scarlet Letter.*

Many myths and legends surround this old burying ground and one of the children's favorite is that of the notorious pirate Captain Kidd. He was supposedly buried here after being hung in England. How he got here is anybody's guess, but for a long time, children were told if they knocked on one of the stones three times and whispered, "Captain Kidd, for what were you hung?" Captain Kidd would answer . . . nothing (of course!).

The oldest stone here is that of William Paddy, dated 1658. It pays tribute to this fine old Puritan—if you can decipher it: "Here sleaps Hat / Blessed one Whoes Lief / God Help us all to Live / That so when we this World Must / Leve / We Ever May Be Happy / With Blessed William Paddy."

➨ **Directions to King's Chapel Burying Ground:** King's Chapel is on the corner of Tremont and School streets in downtown Boston. The burying ground is adjacent to the chapel.

Granary Burying Ground
Tremont Street

The "Old Granary" is on the opposite side of Tremont Street from King's Chapel (about one block away) and is entered through large stone gates. It takes its name from a wooden granary that, during colonial days, stood next to it. Dating back to 1660, this old cemetery has been known as "the burying ground of the patriots." Just inside the gates to the right is a large rough stone marking the graves of the five victims of the Boston Massacre, among them Crispus Attucks (c.1723–1770), a former slave.

Three signers of the Declaration of Independence are buried here: John Hancock (1736–1793), who was also the first governor of Massachusetts; Samuel Adams (1722–1803), who was the second governor, and Robert Treat Paine (1731–1814). When Hancock died, his body lay in state for eight days, and a long parade of dignitaries followed the bier to the cemetery. It was said, at that time, to be "one of the greatest funeral pageants Boston had seen." It is also said that Hancock's devoted servant Frank lies buried at his side, noted only by his first name.

Paul Revere (1735–1818), who made his famous ride to alert the Minutemen that the British were coming, is buried here, with an impressive monument denoting his grave site.

A large memorial structure in the center of the cemetery is a memorial to the parents of Benjamin Franklin, whose home was not far from this site. A long epitaph on its face (written by Franklin) ends with, "He was a pious and prudent man; She a discreet and virtuous woman."

Ann Pollard (1620–1725), the first woman to land in Boston, is also buried here. She lived to be 105, and

The landmark gravesite of revolutionary Paul Revere at Granary Burying Ground in Boston.

when she died, more than 135 of her descendants attended her funeral, as well as a large contingent of Harvard students. She was the proprietor of the former Horse Shoe Tavern, just around the corner on Beacon Street, which was a favorite haunt of Harvard students. Her great-grandchild Robbie, who had died a few days previously, was laid in her arms for burial.

But, with all due respect to the patriots, statesmen, governors and early settlers, the most popular grave site in this cemetery is that of the following:

"Mother Goose"
1665–1757

No one knows for sure just who the real Mother Goose was, but to the thousands of children who have visited the Old Granary over the years she was a kindly grandmother who lived in nearby Pudding Lane (now Devonshire Street) and who made up lots of wonderful ditties. After all, she was buried here and has a tombstone to prove it—even though it says, "Here Lyes Ye Body of Mary Goose."

Believing that Boston's Mother Goose is buried here requires a leap of faith, for this is actually the grave site of Mary Goose, and probably that of Elizabeth and Isaac Goose, as well!

The legend began with Elizabeth Foster, who was born in Boston in 1665 and who in 1690 married the widower Isaac Goose (né Vergoose), who had ten children. (His first wife, Mary, died in 1690.) Elizabeth and Isaac proceeded to have ten more children. But unlike the old women who lived in a shoe, Elizabeth knew just what to do with them—she entertained them with little songs and ditties that she made up.

Years later, after her husband passed away, she went to live with her daughter, also named Elizabeth, who had married Thomas Fleet, a prosperous Boston printer. She was a much-welcomed addition to the household as the Fleets now had 14 children of their own who demanded a good deal of attention. Right at home with this big brood, "Mother Goose," as she was then called, continued her old habit by entertaining her grandchildren with her repertoire. Her son-in-law was so charmed by her collection of songs and verse that he decided to put them into print. They were made into a book called *Mother Goose's Melodies for Children*.

Mother Goose died at the ripe old age of 92 in 1757, and it is assumed that she is buried in the same grave (as was often the custom) as Isaac and his first wife, Mary. On the map just inside the burying ground gates, however, are directions for finding the grave of "Mother Goose." (See photograph on page 1).

➤➤ **Directions to Granary Burying Ground:** Next to the Park Street Church on Tremont Street (one block south and on the opposite side of the street from King's Chapel Burying Ground). Directions to the grave sites are displayed on a map inside the gates.

Central Burying Ground
Boston Common (south side)

This burying ground, located on the south side of the Boston Common, was opened in 1756. Over the years, a number of the bodies originally buried here were exhumed for one reason or another, mostly due to the expansion of Boylston Street. Many of the graves are unmarked, including those of both British and American soldiers (the former, victims of Bunker Hill; the latter, laid low by disease incurred during the Siege of Boston) who were buried side by side in a common grave. Irish Catholic immigrants with the inscription "Strangers" are buried here as well. Gilbert Stuart (1755–1828), the artist famous for his portraits of George and Martha Washington, lies here, and it is believed that Mary Dyer (d.1660), a Quaker who was hung on the common for her beliefs, is also buried here. (A statue of her stands in front of the statehouse.)

➤➤ **Directions to Central Burying Ground:** The cemetery is on the southeast corner of Boston Common, near Boylston Street. (This cemetery is enclosed by an iron fence and is usually kept locked. For entrance and more information, call the Boston Parks rangers, who offer guided tours; 617-725-4505.)

Copp's Hill Burying Ground
Hull Street

Copp's Hill is Boston's second oldest cemetery and is located in the historic North End. It has become famous for its antique stones and curious epitaphs more than for its inhabitants. (Some stones still bear the marks of being used for target practice by British troops during the Battle of Bunker Hill.) Many of the names of those buried here have long since vanished into obscurity. One family name, however, has not, and that marks the tomb of "The Reverent Doctors Increase, Cotton & Samuel Mather" and their descendants.

The Mather Family Tomb
c.1639–1728

Increase Mather (1639–1723) was the leading clergyman of the Puritans and, as such, exerted tremendous influence over the colony. He was president of Harvard College from 1685 to 1701 and was a prolific writer. It was he who influenced the then-governor, Sir William Phipps, to institute the infamous Salem Witch Trials in 1692. His son, Cotton Mather (1663–1728), followed in his footsteps as minister, joining him as co-pastor of Boston's Second Church. When Cotton was rejected as a contender for the presidency of Harvard College, however, he stormed off in a rage and helped found Yale in 1703. He is mostly remembered for his writings, which in 1692 helped to incite the wave of hysterical fear that resulted in the Salem Witch Trials. After six months of trials in which 20 people were hung (one was pressed to death by weights), both Cotton and Increase recanted their ideas and called for an end to the trials.

Also buried in the family tomb is Hannah Mather Crocker (1752–1829), granddaughter and great-granddaughter of the "Puritan divines" and a writer. In 1818 she wrote one of the earliest feminist tracts in America, *Observations on the Real Rights of Women*.

➤ **Directions to Copp's Hill Burying Ground:** In the North End of Boston, on Hull Street near the Old North Church, on the Freedom Trail. The Mather Family tomb is in the southeast corner.

Phipps Street Burying Grounds
Phipps Street (Charlestown)

One monument stands out among the rest in this very old cemetery, the third oldest in Boston, and it is that of John Harvard (d.1637), for whom Harvard College is named. Not much is known of John, although a very popular statue of him was erected in Harvard Yard (in spite of the fact that no one knows what he looked like). He was a clergyman, educated in England, who died within a year of arriving in Boston. In his will he left all his books and half of his fortune, about £395, to the new school then being founded. His benefactors were so impressed with this exceptional legacy that they named the school in his honor.

➤➤ **Directions to Phipps Street Burying Grounds:** Phipps Street is four blocks north of Thompson Square Triangle. The cemetery is at the end of the street. Unfortunately, this cemetery is kept locked at all times due to vandalism, but you may call the Cemetery Department of the Boston Parks and Recreation Department, 617-725-4505, for special arrangements to visit the cemetery.

Mount Hope Cemetery
355 Walk Hill Street (Hyde Park)

Hyde Park, one of Boston's "neighborhoods," was incorporated in 1868, and it became a popular area for writers, artists and reformers of the day. Many of them are buried in Mount Hope Cemetery, and the two best remembered, particularly for their work in the abolitionist and women's rights movements, are the Grimke sisters.

Sarah Grimke
1792–1873
Angelina Grimke
1805–1879

Originally from Charleston, South Carolina, and brought up in an upper-class, slave-owning family, they became disturbed over what was to them the immorality of slavery. In the late 1820s, the sisters moved north, first to Philadelphia and then to Boston, vowing never to live in the south again. They became among the first women to speak out against slavery and the first to speak to "mixed" audiences, consisting of both men and women. The strong objections to their appearances in public (women just didn't do that in the 1820s) made them strong advocates of women's rights as well.

Also buried here is Susanna Rowson (c.1762–1824), whose novel *Charlotte Temple* (written in 1792) is claimed to be America's first best-seller, and Michael J. "King" Kelly (1857–1894), the baseball great immortalized in the song "Slide, Kelly, Slide."

➼ **Directions to Mount Hope Cemetery:** Approximately, 5 miles (south) from downtown Boston on Route 1 to Hyde Park Avenue, turn east on Walk Hill Road. Mount Hope is on the north side of Forest Hills Cemetery.

Forest Hills Cemetery
Morton Street (Jamaica Plain)

A far cry from the old, overcrowded cemeteries of colonial Boston is the rural, or "garden," cemetery that came into vogue at the beginning of the 19th century (see Mount Auburn Cemetery in Cambridge, Massachusetts). Forest Hills, with its 260 acres of manicured lawns and shrubs surrounding a scenic lake and dotted with imposing statuary and monuments, is just such a place.

Inside the elaborate front gates a map shows where to find the graves of distinguished men and women who are buried here, such as Eugene O'Neill (1888–1953), a winner of the Nobel Prize for literature and four-time winner of the Pulitzer Prize for drama; e. e. cummings (1894–1962), known for his eccentric style of poetry; William Jennings Bryan (1860–1925), famed orator and attorney; Edward Everett Hale (1822–1909), clergyman and author; William Lloyd Garrison (1805–1879), the fiery abolitionist; and Emily G. Balch (1867–1961), whose life was devoted to promoting world peace and who was the second American woman to win the Nobel Prize for peace.

The first crematory in New England was established here in 1893. Lucy Stone, a leader in many ways, was the first person in New England to be cremated.

Lucy Stone
1818–1893

A leader in the early struggle for women's rights, Lucy Stone came from one of New England's first families. She was born in 1818 on a farm near Brookfield, Massachusetts, the eighth of nine brothers and sisters.

In 1847, at a time when few women were allowed to attend college or to speak out in public, she graduated with high honors from Oberlin College (refusing to write the commencement address, because she would not have been permitted to read it). She then went on to become the first woman to lecture publicly.

When she married Henry Blackwell, an ardent abolitionist, in 1855, she not only drew up her own marriage contract but insisted on keeping her own name. (Thereafter, a woman who kept her maiden name was often called "a Lucy Stoner.") She dedicated her life to women's causes and is particularly remembered for founding the *Woman's Journal,* a highly respected publication that was considered "the voice of the woman's movement."

Just before she died of a stomach tumor on October 18, 1893, she whispered to her only daughter, Alice, "Make the world better." Lucy had made detailed preparations for her funeral, including cremation and, in her husband's words, "was in death as in life, a pioneer—the first person in Massachusetts to be cremated." A simple service was held at the Church of the Disciples in Dorchester, and it was noted in the *Woman's Journal:* "It would have been a complete surprise to her gentle spirit to see hundreds of people standing silent in the street waiting for the doors to be opened." More than 1,100 people crowded into the church, and many had to stand.

Years later, her husband's and daughter's ashes were mingled with hers and now repose in a large copper urn (under the name Blackwell) in the Crematory at Forest Hills.

➤ **Directions to Forest Hills Cemetery:** The cemetery is approximately 5 miles south of downtown Boston by car via the Jamaicaway (Route 1) to Morton Street (Route 203). A map to the cemetery, indicating prominent grave sites, is just inside the gates.

Nicola Sacco
1891–1927
Bartolomeo Vanzetti
1888–1927

The names of Sacco and Vanzetti have been indelibly linked in the annals of American justice since 1920. On April 15 of that year a payroll robbery took place in Braintree, Massachusetts, in which two men were killed. Nicolla Sacco, a shoemaker, and Bartolomeo Vanzetti, a fish peddler, both Italian immigrants and anarchists, were accused of the crime. They were tried at the Dedham courthouse, found guilty and sentenced to death by electrocution. The trial, held at a time when there was great hostility toward aliens and radicals in this country, became a cause célèbre both here and abroad. It was believed by many that the two men had been tried and convicted for their political beliefs rather than the crime itself.

Sacco and Vanzetti were executed at the Charlestown State Prison (now demolished) at midnight on August 22, 1927. Emotions ran so high on that day and into the night that 800 police officers were dispatched to surround the prison, and the entire area was roped off for a distance of $\frac{1}{2}$ mile.

At midnight, Sacco was led from his death cell to the electric chair, and as he was being strapped in he shouted in Italian, "Long live anarchy!" Just as the switch was pulled, however, he was heard to cry out the word *mama*. A few minutes later, Vanzetti was led to the chair, and as he was strapped in he said in English, "I now wish to forgive some people for what they are doing to me."

Both bodies were taken to the Langone Funeral Home at the foot of Hanover Street in Boston's North End, where they were to lie in state for four days. Approximately 100,000 people filed through the small funeral parlor (so many that the terrazzo floor and the marble threshold began to crack).

On the fifth day, the funeral procession began to form at North End Park near the Paul Revere House. With 500 police officers patrolling the area, four open cars heaped with flowers preceded the two hearses carrying the bodies and two limousines carrying the family. Countless friends, struggling under the weight of huge floral pieces, entered the cortege, followed by more than 5,000 marchers.

Along the 6-mile route to Forest Hills Crematory in Jamaica Plain, where the two bodies would be cremated, 200,000 people watched the procession (later called the "March of Sorrow") pass by, and when it arrived at Forest Hills, several thousand more who had arrived earlier crowded the grassy area surrounding the small chapel.

What became of the ashes of the two men remained a well-kept secret for many years. It was eventually learned that their ashes, along with their death masks, were safely stored away at the Boston Public Library.

Mount Calvary Cemetery
Cummins Highway (West Roxbury)

Mount Calvary, New Calvary, Calvary, and Mount Hope cemeteries are adjacent to one another in the Forest Hills section of Boston near the Arnold Arboretum and Franklin Park. In these hallowed grounds lie a whole new generation of prominent Bostonians who have left their mark on the city.

James Michael Curley
1874–1958

James Michael Curley was one of Boston's most colorful politicians. When he died in 1958, John F. Kennedy, then U.S. Senator from Massachusetts, summed up his life with the words, "[His] fabulous and fascinating career of more than half a century reflected in many ways the life and growth of the city he loved."

Curley held sway in both state and city politics from the beginning to the middle of the 20th century, serving four terms in the U.S. House of Representatives, one term as governor of Massachusetts and four terms as mayor of Boston—winning his last term while imprisoned on a mail-fraud conviction.

More than 100,000 ("a human tide") filed by the Curley bier in the Hall of Flags in the state capitol, where his body lay in state for three days (only the third person so honored up to that time). When the cortege moved from the capitol to the Holy Cross Cathedral for services, and then on to Mount Calvary Cemetery, an estimated 500,000 people lined the roadways, the largest crowd ever seen in Boston. *The Boston Globe* said it was the "greatest tribute ever accorded a public figure in this city."

➤➤ **Directions to Mount Calvary Cemetery:** The J. M. Curley grave site is on Chapel Path (southwest), next to the chapel (enter the cemetery on Mount Calvary Avenue, which is off Cummins Highway).

New Calvary Cemetery
800 Harvard Street (Mattapan)

The New Calvary Cemetery is an extension of the Mount Calvary Cemetery, and this is where John Lawrence Sullivan (1858–1918)—"the great John L." is buried. The man who boasted he could "lick any man in the world" dominated professional boxing from 1882 until 1892. He toured the United States and Europe and, with his bare knuckles, would challenge anyone who cared to enter the ring with him. (He knocked out 59 men in succession during one exhibition.) His flamboyant personality and life-style made John L. a favorite with American sports fans, even after he was finally defeated by "Gentleman Jim" Corbet in 1892. Shortly after Sullivan retired, he renounced his old life-style and became a temperance advocate.

John Michael Casey (d.1959) is also buried in this cemetery. He was the first official stage censor in Boston and the one whose notorious stamp of disapproval, "Banned in Boston," succeeded in bringing the curtain down on many theatricals in this city over the course of 28 years (1904–1932).

➤➤ **Directions to New Calvary Cemetery:** See Mount Calvary Cemetery. J. L. Sullivan's grave site in on Honeysuckle Path; J. M. Casey's is on Chapel Avenue.

St. Joseph's Cemetery
990 LaGrange Street (West Roxbury)

Two of Boston's most charismatic native sons are buried here in this large, modern Catholic cemetery: the beloved "Music Man," Arthur Fiedler, and "Honey Fitz," the grandfather of John F. Kennedy, John Francis Fitzgerald.

Arthur Fiedler
1894–1979

Tributes poured in from around the world on the day that Boston's beloved Music Man, Arthur Fiedler, died of a heart attack at age 84. The world-famous conductor of the Boston Pops for half a century was heralded as "a Boston institution," "as much a part of Boston as the swan boats and the Old North Church" and "the first citizen of the musical entertainment world."

Four days later, 125,000 people crowded the banks of the Charles River to pay their last respects to the late maestro. A special memorial was held in his honor at the Hatch Shell—a repeat of Fiedler's stirring Bicentennial Program of July 4, 1976. Just before 9 P.M., assistant conductor of the Pops and esteemed friend of the late conductor, Harry Ellis Dickson, walked quietly away from the podium. Softly at first, the musicians, without a conductor, began to play the opening strains of John Philip Sousa's "Stars and Stripes Forever," but as they picked up the tempo, the crowd, as so often before, rose to its feet and began to clap rhythmically in unison. This time, however, the music took on a tremendous emotional fervor. As the American flag unfurled and a flurry of fireworks broke overhead, the crowd broke into thunderous applause. It was one of the most stirring memorials to a Boston superstar the town had ever witnessed.

John F. "Honey Fitz" Fitzgerald
1863–1956

John F. Fitzgerald was one of the most popular mayors of Boston, and a powerful state Democrat. But he is also well known as the colorful and much-loved grandfather of President John F. Kennedy. He died at the age of 87 after a long illness, and the flags around the city were lowered to half mast. The Holy Cross Cathedral was filled to capacity with dignitaries of the city, state and nation, including every living ex-mayor of the city. Thousands more lined the streets and watched the cortege move through the city en route to St. Joseph's Cemetery, where an estimated 3,500 attended the burial serivce at the grave site.

➡ **Directions to St. Joseph's Cemetery:** From Boston take Route 9 west to Newton; turn south at Hammond Street; LaGrange Street (about 1 mile) is a right (west) turn. St. Joseph's Cemetery is across the street from Mount Benedict Cemetery.

Brookline   *Holyhood Cemetery*
Heath Street

Joseph P. Kennedy
1888–1969

It was called "the death of a dynasty" when Joseph P. Kennedy, age 81, died of a heart attack at his summer home at Hyannis Port, Massachusetts. The former U.S. ambassador to Great Britain from 1938 to 1940 and "founding father of the nation's most glittering and star-crossed political dynasty" saw each of his four sons rise to high achievements—one a U.S. president, one an attorney general, another a U.S. senator and yet another a World War II hero.

At a private Catholic Mass at St. Xavier's church in Hyannis Port for about 50 family members and close friends, many of his grandchildren took part in the special service, reading psalms and carrying the offertory gifts to the altar. His flag-draped coffin was then taken by hearse to the cemetery in Brookline, 75 miles away, to be buried in the family plot. The press and public were barred from the grounds (to protect the other graves) during the simple grave site service in which his son Senator Edward Kennedy gave the eulogy. A large granite family stone marks the site, with several smaller headstones denoting the graves of other family members. Fresh flowers are often placed here. (His two assassinated sons, John and Robert, are buried in Arlington National Cemetery.)

James B. Connolly (1868–1957), who claimed the title of "the first modern Olympic champion," winning the first Olympic medal in the 1896 games by leaping 45 feet in the hop, skip and jump, is also buried in this cemetery.

➤➤ **Directions to Holyhood Cemetery:** From Boston, take Route 9 west to Newton; turn south onto Hammond Street; the first street on the right (west) is Heath Street. The Kennedy grave site is toward the back on the corner of O'Connell Avenue. The Connolly grave is along a path on the east side of the cemetery.

Mount Auburn Cemetery Cambridge
580 Mount Auburn Street

In the early 1800s, "proper" Bostonians were beginning to have second thoughts about their quaint old city graveyards, deeming them "injurious to health" and "repulsive to the taste of a refined age." Dr. Jacob Bigelow (1789–1879), a physician and Harvard teacher as well as a botanist, conceived the idea of the "rural" cemetery, or "garden" cemetery, for commemoration of notable individuals. Along with Henry A. S. Dearborn (1751–1829), the first president of the Massachusetts Horticultural Society, Bigelow acquired 72 acres of hilly woodland on the Charles River in Cambridge. They called it Mount Auburn, the first garden cemetery in America, and it was to be the prototype of cemetery design across the country for years to come.

Today, Mount Auburn Cemetery (called by some the "Valhalla of Boston") encompasses 172 acres of beautifully landscaped gardens, roads and paths that conform to the natural terrain; reflecting lakes and ponds and artful statuary and monuments. It has become a haven for migrating birds as well as the deceased, and early-morning bird-watchers are given their own keys to the imposing Egyptian-style entrance gates. At the front office you can obtain a number of brochures about the cemetery, including the *Roll of Distinction,* which lists and gives locations for the grave sites of at least 450 noted persons interred here. Among the famous are Henry Wadsworth Longfellow (1807–1882), Oliver Wendell Holmes (1809–1894), Winslow Homer (1836–1910), Julia Ward Howe (1819–1910), Fannie Farmer (1857–1915), Edwin Booth (1833–1893), Charlotte Cushman (1816–1876), Henry Cabot Lodge (1850–1924), James Russell Lowell (1819–1891), Amy Lowell (1874–1925), Charles Sumner (1811–1874), Mary Baker Eddy (1821–1910), Isabella Stewart Gardner (1840–1924), Dorothea Dix (1802–1887) and almost every Harvard president since 1810.

The funerals for some of these people were conducted with much pomp and ceremony, whereas the funerals of others were simple, quiet affairs. One of the more memorable ones recorded was that of Charles Sumner, the popular statesman and abolitionist. When he was fatally stricken with a heart attack in the U.S. Senate and then brought back to Boston for memorial services at King's Chapel, the procession of mourners that accompanied the body from King's Chapel to Mount Auburn Cemetery was more than 1 mile long. Leaders from every branch of government and every institution in the state marched along with hundreds of African-American citizens from all walks of life in gratitude for his efforts on their behalf. Nearby church bells tolled mournfully as the procession passed thousands of spectators along the 4-mile route and thousands more stood on the hills and around the gates of the cemetery to pay their last respects to this beloved citizen.

Another venerated Bostonian, Julia Ward Howe, called the "Dearest Old Lady in America," was the author of the "Battle Hymn of the Republic" and was buried with great ceremony. She lies next to her husband, Samuel Gridley Howe (1801–1876), who was the director of the Perkins School for the Blind. When she died of pneumonia at the age of 91, the governor of Massachusetts led the dignitaries at her funeral. A special memorial service was held in the packed Boston Symphony Hall, and hundreds more of her admirers had to be turned away. At the close of the service, more than 4,000 people joined in singing the "Battle Hymn of the Republic."

Mary Baker Eddy, founder of the Church of Christ Scientist and the *Christian Science Monitor,* has one of the most beautiful memorials in the cemetery. When she died of "natural causes" in 1910, preparations for her funeral were kept as quiet and as secret as possible to keep the thousands of curious away from the cemetery. A simple ceremony was held at her home in Chestnut Hill with only about 100 in attendance, and then her bronze casket (with a small window on the top for viewing the body) was taken to Mount Auburn Cemetery and placed in a temporary tomb. (Much has been made of the "telephone" in her tomb, which was put there for a few days for the guards who watched over her grave site in anticipation of unwanted visitors. It was never needed.) Her casket was eventually moved to its present site—under an elaborate monument of eight tall, white fluted columns encircling the tomb, which is blanketed with pink and white flowers in season. Carved on the memorial are the words "Mary Baker Eddy, discoverer and founder of Christian Science. Author of Science and Health with Key to the Scriptures."

Another famous Boston woman, Isabella Stewart Gardner, better known as "Mrs. Jack," the renowned art collector, is buried in the family mausoleum. However, her home, Fenway Court in Boston's Back Bay, one of Boston's most treasured museums, is considered her living memorial. When she died of a severe attack of angina at the age of 85, an Episcopal service was held in the chapel of Fenway Court. Her will imposed very rigid terms demanding that every item in the museum must remain in its original place; and so it is to this day (except for several unrecovered valuable paintings that were stolen in a dramatic heist in 1990).

➤➤ **Directions to Mount Auburn Cemetery:** The cemetery, located on Mount Auburn Street, is about 1 mile north of Harvard Square on the Cambridge–Watertown line. It is open daily from 8:00 A.M. to 7:00 P.M. (closing at 4:30 in the winter), and a map to the famous grave sites is available in the office.

City of Cambridge Cemetery
76 Coolidge Avenue

Henry James
1843–1916

Although born in New York and educated at Harvard, Henry James spent most of his life in London, England. Considered an American novelist and short-story writer, James became a British citizen in 1915, a year before his death. His novels drew sharp and critical comparisons between the refined British and what he considered less-cultured American ways. *The American* (1877), *Daisy Miller* (1879), *The Golden Bowl* (1904) and *The Turn of the Screw* (1898) are regarded among his finest work. He died in London of a series of paralytic strokes, and his last words were said to be, "Tell the boys to follow, to be faithful, to take me seriously." After a funeral service at the Old Chelsea Church in London, his body was cremated and the ashes returned to America to be buried in the family plot in Cambridge.

Next to Henry James's tombstone is an identical one for his brother, William James (1842–1910), Harvard University psychologist and philosopher, who had died six years before him. William James, however, is not buried here. He died at his home in Chocorua, New Hampshire, from heart problems at the age of 73, and his body was brought to Cambridge for a memorial service in the Appleton Chapel in nearby Harvard Yard. After the service, his body was cremated and the ashes returned to Chocorua to be scattered in a mountain stream.

In the same area as the James family plot is the grave

of a highly respected editor and writer of his day, William Dean Howells (1837–1920). Among his many novels, *The Rise of Silas Lapham* (1885) was required reading for many generations of American high school students.

➤➤ **Directions to City of Cambridge Cemetery:** Coolidge Avenue is off Mount Auburn Street bordering the Mount Auburn Cemetery (see directions). After entering the main gates follow the road to the right all the way toward the back of the cemetery to the red brick wall on the left. All three stones are in this area.

Milton Cemetery **Milton**
Centre Street

Howard D. Johnson
1896–1972

For several generations, the name of Howard Johnson (or "HoJos") has been a welcome sign along the highway for hungry American families. Since the early 1930s the familiar restaurant with the orange tile roof and blue trim meant good food at reasonable prices and a place where children were treated as equals. But best of all, it meant ice cream in 28 delicious flavors.

Howard Johnson began his business career at the age of 24 when he inherited his father's debt-ridden cigar store in Wollaston (part of Quincy). Through hard work he was able to turn it around. His big success came, however, from his love of ice cream. He bought a recipe from a German pushcart vendor, which called for doubling the butterfat content of ordinary ice cream and adding only natural flavors. It became so popular that Johnson was soon opening beach stands from Wollaston to Cape Cod to sell his ice cream. He eventually opened a chain of restaurants, followed by motels and snack shops, all carrying the familiar blue-and-orange packaged products. His concept of training individuals to run their own restaurants while he retained control over the quality of the products became the model for many restaurant franchise businesses.

A large, well-attended funeral service was held at the First Parish Church in Milton, and he was buried in Milton Cemetery.

➤ **Directions to Milton Cemetery:** The cemetery is at the intersection of Centre Street and Randolph Avenue (Route 28).

Quincy *The United First Parish Church*
1306 Hancock Street

Abigail Adams
1744–1818
John Adams
1735–1826
John Quincy Adams
1767–1848

The United First Parish Church in Quincy is referred to by local townspeople as the "Church of the Presidents," and rightly so. For it is here in this handsome Quincy granite structure in the center of town that two presidents of the United States, John Adams and John Quincy Adams, and their wives are buried side by side in vaults in the grotto of the church.

Abigail, a strong influence on both her husband and son (her husband referred to her as "his fellow Labourer") preceded her husband in death and was the first to be buried here. She died on October 28, 1818, of typhoid fever, and many dignitaries walked in the procession from the Adamses' home, several blocks away, to the church. Of all the eloquent tributes paid to her at the time of her death, perhaps none was so touching as the one by her son John Quincy, who wrote, "Her life gave the lie to every libel on her sex that was ever written."

John Adams died seven years later on the Fourth of July, 1826, the 50th anniversary of the Declaration of Independence. A few days before his death, one of the leading men of Quincy had called on the ailing 91-year-old former president and asked him if he would give a toast that could be presented at the coming celebration. "Independence Forever!" was Adam's quick, firm reply. A few days later, on his deathbed he whispered his last words, "Thomas Jefferson survives." Ironically, however, Jefferson had preceded him in death by just 3 hours. A marble tablet placed next to his tomb is inscribed: "On the Fourth of July 1826 / He was summoned / To the Independence of Immortality / And to the JUDGMENT OF HIS GOD."

John Quincy Adams suffered a heart attack on the floor of the House of Representatives (he had served in the House for 17 years following his term as president) on February 21, 1848. His colleagues quickly placed him on a sofa and moved him to the Speaker's Room, where he remained for two days in a semiconscious state. During this time Congress assembled in respectful silence and then immediately adjourned from day to day. On the evening of the second day John Quincy Adams murmured, "This is the end of the earth, but I am composed," then he slipped into a final coma and died.

The funeral took place in the Washington, D.C., on February 26, "taking on the air," as one pundit wrote, "of a national pageant, with frequent cannon salutes, tolling of bells, marching military companies, funeral bands, tons of crepe paper, and long lines of mourners." The casket was transported to Quincy, where J. Q. Adams was buried in the family crypt next to his father and mother. (Four years later, his wife, Louisa, was laid to rest at his side.)

➼ **Directions to The United First Parish Church:** From Route 93, take exit 8 to the center of Quincy, where the United First Parish Church is located. Call the church for tours and information: 617-773-1290.

Newton

Newton Cemetery
791 Walnut Street

Another very attractive garden cemetery in the Boston area is the Newton Cemetery, and there are many exceptionally creative people buried here.

Margaret Knight (1838–1914) was one of the very first woman inventors in this country, with more than 30 patents to her credit. Many of her inventions, including a paper bag folding machine, required the use of heavy machinery—which in 1870 was not considered the type of work for a woman to do.

Francis Stanley (1849–1918) was the identical twin of Freelan Stanley (see Kingfield, Maine), and together they invented the famous "Stanley Steamer" automobile. It was the first automobile to reach the top of Mount Washington (1899)—and the climb was accomplished in 2 hours and 10 minutes.

Percy L. Spencer (1895–1970) invented something dear to the hearts of the modern generation—the microwave oven. Working in the lab at Raytheon Manufacturing Company one day, he reached into his pocket for a candy bar and, to his amazement, found that it had melted. He quickly discovered the cause; he had also put a small tube in his pocket, a magnetron that produced microwaves—and instant cooking!

Louis K. Liggett (1875–1946), founder of a popular chain of drugstores, is buried here in a large, mausoleum. Louis Fabian Bachrach (1881–1963), esteemed photographer of the rich and famous, has a magnificent monument with a bronze sculpture of a weeping angel in the center marking his grave site.

One of the favorite stones in the cemetery is the one on a large granite tomb that says in bold letters "Author of My Country 'Tis of Thee." It is the grave site of Samuel Francis Smith (1808–1895), a Baptist clergyman and poet who wrote the national hymn "America" while he was a student at Andover Theological Seminary.

➤ **Directions to Newton Cemetery:** From Newton Center, go west on Beacon Street to Walnut Street and turn right. The entrance to the cemetery will be immediately on your left. Information can be obtained at the office, although most of the stones are along the roadways.

Effie Canning Carlton
1856–1940

The name of Effie Calton may not sound familiar, but the song she wrote definitely is. Surely no house in this country is a stranger to the words and tune of "Rock-a-Bye-Baby."

One day while trying to quiet a neighbor's baby, Effie Crocker, age 14, started rocking him and singing a little tune that she made up as she went along. It worked so well that she wrote it down. Later, she played the song for her piano teacher, who was so impressed that she sent Effie off to play it for a music publisher. When he told Effie he wanted to publish her song, she was afraid that her father might not approve, so she gave her name as Effie Canning (her grandmother's name). The song was an instant success and became popular throughout the world.

Just below her name on her tombstone are the words "Composer of 'Rock-a-Bye-Baby'." (According

The gravestone of Effie C. Carlton at Mount Feake Cemetery in Waltham.

to Bartlett's *Familiar Quotations,* similar words are attributed to Charles Dupee Blake, 1846–1903.)

➤➤ **Directions to Mount Feake Cemetery:** From Waltham center, go west on Main Street (Route 20), turn south on Prospect Street; the cemetery is about 1 mile on the west side of the street. The grave site is along the road on the south side of the river.

Natick   *Glenwood Cemetery*
Glenwood Street (South Natick)

Horatio Alger
1834–1899

Horatio Alger graduated from Harvard Divinity School in 1860 and had planned to follow in his father's footsteps as a Unitarian minister. But the stories he wrote for young boys became so popular Alger left the ministry and became a professional writer. All of his stories followed the "rags to riches" theme, involving young boys whose determination to overcome poverty and adversity brought rich rewards in the end. Alger wrote more than 100 such novels, and they were so widely read that the term Horatio Alger came to define anyone who overcame poverty and rose to a high position.

Alger continued to write until he died of a heart ailment in 1899, and several more of his books were published posthumously. According to the author's wishes, his body was cremated and a simple memorial service with a brief eulogy was held in the Eliot Unitarian Church in South Natick. He is buried in the family plot in the nearby Glenwood Cemetery, the site marked by a large granite family tombstone.

➤➤ **Directions to Glenwood Cemetery:** From South Natick center (Route 16), turn east onto Glenwood Street; the cemetery is a short distance. The Alger grave site is in the northwest corner.

This old cemetery close to the center of the village was once an area of verdant fields and hills where the literati of Concord strolled. Today, it is the final resting place for many of them, and as such is a popular tourist attraction. So popular, in fact, that tour buses often pull into its small parking area and stop by a sign that reads, "Author's Ridge." Arrows point the way to the grave sites of the famous Concord authors—Louisa May Alcott (1832–1888), Ralph Waldo Emerson (1803–1882), Nathanial Hawthorne (1804–1864) and Henry David Thoreau (1817–1862)—all buried within a short distance of one another.

Devotees make the pilgrimage here throughout the year and bring flowers for the graves. Even in the dead of winter, it is not uncommon to find small bouquets of pine and spruce boughs placed with care on the snow-covered grave of Louisa May Alcott or a cluster of pine cones on Thoreau's grave. The stones that mark these graves are small, quite ordinary and without epitaph. Only Emerson's stands out from the rest; a large rough boulder with a bronze plaque inscribed with the words "The passive master lent his hand to the vast soul that o'er him planned." Close by Emerson's grave is that of his favorite aunt, Mary Moody Emerson, whose stone bears an epitaph written by Emerson.

Louisa May Alcott's gravesite at Sleepy Hollow Cemetery in Concord.

Mary Moody Emerson
1774–1863

Mary Moody Emerson, born in Concord and descended from a long line of New England ministers, was called the "eccentric but brilliant" aunt of the renowned poet and essayist Ralph Waldo Emerson.

When her brother, William, minister of the First Church in Boston, died in 1811, Mary immediately went to the aid of his widow, who was left with six children. She devoted herself to their education, particularly the boys. Ralph Waldo soon became her favorite, and during his formative years, her moral advice and constant urging to "Scorn trifles, lift your aims: do what you are afraid to do," was to set the pattern of his independent thinking.

Mary had what was called "a keen and inquiring mind" and was considered one of the best-educated women of her day. She had a strong influence not only on her nephew but on many young men of Concord, including another budding intellectual, Henry David Thoreau.

As she aged, Mary became quite eccentric, and many stories are told of her making her own shroud and "wearing it night and day." As a strong Calvinist, she believed that death was the climax of life. She talked about "the dear worms" as she waited for death, but when it didn't come (according to a neighbor), "it was unthinkable to a thrifty New Englander, that a whole garment should remain unused, even a shroud, so she took to wearing it, first as a nightgown, then out of doors."

Mary Moody Emerson lived to be 88 years old, and when at last she died, she was buried in the Sleepy Hollow Cemetery, next to those she loved. The inscription on her stone was taken from the closing lines of the essay that Emerson wrote about her: "She gave high counsels—it was the privilege of certain boys to have this immeasurably high standard indicated to their childhoods, a blessing which nothing else in education could supply."

Also buried in this cemetery is the noted American sculptor Daniel Chester French (1850–1931), best known for his statue of the seated Lincoln in Washington, D.C., and the Minuteman statue on the Battleground in Concord. The ashes of the German-American modern architect Walter Gropius (1883–1969) are said to have been scattered in this cemetery.

➤➤ **Directions to Sleepy Hollow Cemetery:** From the center of Concord (Monument Square), turn east onto Court Lane to Bedford Road (Route 62), and the cemetery is just a short distance on the north side of the street. Signs and arrows point the way to "Author's Ridge" and Daniel Chester French's grave.

North of Boston

Famous seaports, early mill towns and old historic villages combine to make the area north of Boston rich in Yankee history. And no visitor of graveyards would want to miss the city of Salem, site of the infamous Witch Trials of 1692. The North Shore has also been home to a number of notable American writers who drew inspiration from this varied landscape. Many are buried in their hometowns.

Pine Grove Cemetery **Lynn**
145 Boston Street

Lydia Pinkham
1819–1883

Lydia Pinkham had become well known among her friends and neighbors as the person to go to when they were sick. She was particularly skilled at curing "women's ailments," and when her husband's business failed, her sons prevailed on her to bottle and sell her "miracle cure."

In 1876, at the age of 57, she founded the Lydia E. Pinkham Medicine Company, brewing her Vegetable Compound for Female Complaints in the kitchen of her home in Lynn. It includes such ingredients as unicorn root, black cohosh, pleurisy root and about 18 percent alcohol—in spite of the fact that Pinkham was a staunch temperance advocate. Even more remarkable, Pinkham solicited and received testimonials from many satisfied leaders of the Women's Christian Temperance Union.

Pinkham's business grew into a $4 million enterprise and her preparation was marketed in 33 countries. Ads claimed the compound cured such ailments as faintness, the blues, sleeplessness and the "I want to be left alone feeling." Pinkham's own picture on the bottle, that of a sweet little lady, was credited as a great factor in the product's success. It was said that hers was "the best-known female face of the nineteenth century."

At the time of Pinkham's death, five months after suffering a paralytic stroke in 1819, the company was grossing about $300,000 a year. For years after her death, advertisements for the Pinkham compound read, "Although dead, she still sends her message of hope to millions of women." The business continued as a family enterprise until 1973, when it was sold by her great-grandsons and was moved to Puerto Rico. The annual sales of the Vegetable Compound were still grossing more than $700,000 at that time.

➤ **Directions to Pine Grove Cemetery:** From Route 107 north, turn west on to Summer Street, to Boston Street. The grave site is in the center of the cemetery on Hackmatack Avenue.

Peabody *Puritan Lawn Cemetery*
185 Lake Street

Puritan Lawn Cemetery is called a memorial park, and as such it is unlike any other cemetery in the Boston area. There are no gravestones, monuments or ornate tombs to be seen. Simple bronze memorials flush with the ground mark each grave. It is in this somber surroundings that one of the most notorious criminals in Boston's history is buried.

Albert H. De Salvo
"The Boston Strangler"
1931–1973

From June 14, 1962, through January 4, 1964, the murder of 13 women in the Boston area terrorized the city and set off one of the most massive manhunts in the history of this country. The victims, ranging in age from 19 to 85, were all single and living alone; each had apparently let the murderer into her apartment without force. Each had been sexually molested, often brutally, and then strangled to death with an item of her own clothing. The person responsible was soon labeled by the media as "The Boston Strangler."

A police dragnet pulled in scores of suspects, but the crimes continued. The FBI and the attorney general of Massachusetts became involved, but to no avail. Finally, in the 18th month, October 1964, a young woman was attacked in a similar fashion to some of the other victims, only she did not die. She was able to identify her attacker—Albert De Salvo—who had been released from prison in April 1962 after serving time for indecent assault. When his picture appeared in the paper, many women came forward and accused him of attempted assaults.

While awaiting trial for attempted assault, De Salvo was admitted to Bridgewater State Hospital for observation. While there, he confessed to another inmate and then a psychiatrist that he was "The Boston Strangler." He later related scores of pertinent details to the police that only the murderer could have known.

But in spite of the fact that he confessed, De Salvo was never brought to trial for any of the stranglings. He was tried for a series of burglaries and sexual assaults and was defended by noted Boston trial attorney F. Lee Bailey. De Salvo was found guilty and sentenced to jail for life. At Walpole State Prison, fellow inmates called him "Silky," an allusion to the nylon stockings he used to murder his victims. Seven years later he was found stabbed to death in his bed in his prison cell at Walpole.

Nine people, mostly family, attended a private service in Chelsea, and he was buried in the Puritan Lawn Cemetery in Peabody. Controversy over whether De

Salvo was the real "Boston Strangler" continues to surface from time to time.

➤ **Directions to Puritan Lawn Cemetery:** The cemetery is located in Peabody just off Route 1 (a large sign is at the entrance). The grave site is located on Endicott Drive near the calumbarium.

Salem

The Burying Point
Charter Street

As you enter this old cemetery, a bronze plaque lists some of the early settlers to the area who are buried here. Many of them came on the *Arbella*, the ship carrying the first Puritans to this country. Two of the most prominent are Simon Bradstreet (1603–1697), an early governor of the Massachusetts Bay Colony, and his wife, Anne Bradstreet (1612–1672). Anne was the first American female poet of distinction. They are buried in a large box tomb under an old gnarled oak tree. In this fitting setting is also the grave of Justice John Hathorne, one of the judges of the Salem Witch Trials.

One of America's first female poets, Anne Bradstreet is buried here with her husband at Burying Point in Salem.

➤ **Directions to The Burying Point:** The Burying Point is a short walk from the visitor's center in downtown Salem where a map of the area is available.

Danvers

Nurse Homestead
149 Pine Street

Rebecca Nurse
1621–1692

In the 17th century, Danvers was known as Salem Village, and it was here in the winter of 1691 that the infamous Salem Witch Trials began. A group of young girls, listening to the lurid tales of a slave girl, Tituba, began to act as if possessed. They began to accuse women in the neighborhood of being witches, and a mass hysteria ensued in the village.

Among many others, Rebecca Nurse, a devoutly pious, frail 71-year-old matriarch of a large family, was accused of being a witch. Although 40 of her neighbors signed a petition commending her exemplary character, she was hung as a witch. Following her execution, her children secretly removed her body from its unmarked grave, took it back to their homestead and buried it there.

The Nurse Homestead has been preserved, as well as the small graveyard behind the house. In 1885 the Nurse family erected a memorial to Rebecca, a granite shaft, with an inscription from a poem written by John Greenleaf Whittier: "O Christian Martyr, who for truth could die / When all about thee owned the hideous lie, / The world, redeemed from Superstition's sway, / Is breathing freer for thy sake today."

➻ **Directions to Nurse Homestead:** From Route 114, turn north onto Pine Street; the Nurse Homestead is on the corner of Pine and Holten streets; the graveyard is behind the house.

Andover

Andover Chapel Cemetery
Main Street

Harriet Beecher Stowe
1811–1896

It is often quoted that when Harriet Beecher Stowe met Abraham Lincoln, in 1862, the president remarked, "So you're the little woman who wrote the book that made this great war." He was referring, of course, to her novel *Uncle Tom's Cabin,* an antislavery melodrama, which is credited with stirring the nation's consciousness toward the abolitionist cause. Published in 1851, the book sold 300,000 copies within the first year; it was eventually translated into 20 languages and produced as a play on countless stages here and abroad.

Born in Connecticut into the well-known Beecher family of clergymen and educators, she was inspired with ambition and creativity at an early age. When she married a biblical scholar and professor, Calvin Stowe, she began writing to supplement his meager income. *Uncle Tom's Cabin* was written as a result of her moral outrage against the Fugitive Slave Act of 1850. Her later books were not nearly so popular, but she wrote constantly to support her large family, producing an average of a book each year from 1862 to 1884. She completed her autobiography in 1889, just seven years before she died of a stroke at the age of 78. She is buried in the cemetery at Andover Theological Seminary (where her husband taught), between the graves of her husband and her son Henry.

➸ **Directions to Andover Chapel Cemetery:** The seminary, now called Phillips Academy, is on Main Street, a short distance north from the center of town. Turn east at the chapel, and the cemetery is straight ahead on the right behind the school buildings. The Stowe family plot is in the center of the cemetery.

Lowell

Edison Cemetery
Gorham Street

Jack Kerouac
1922–1969

So popular is the grave site of Jack Kerouac, "the king of the beats," that the visitor's center in Lowell has printed a special map to give inquiring visitors. Signs

of the many visitors to the grave site are obvious. In addition to the usual flowers and plants, empty beer cans and wine bottles and cigarette and joint stubs are strewn about or, in some cases, carefully placed. Students like to come here to do grave rubbings of the headstone with its inscription: "He Honored Life."

Kerouac and his friends, particularly the poet Allen Ginsberg, were part of the counterculture (or the "underground poets," as they were called) in the 1950s and 1960s. They ushered in dramatic new changes in American literature. Kerouac's book *On the Road,* describing what was to be dubbed the beatnik life-style, captured the restless spirit of the new generation and became an instant best-seller.

Although he lived a short life, dying from a ruptured hernia in St. Petersburg, Florida, at the age of 47, he left an important and influential body of work. His wife, Stella, brought his body back to his hometown of Lowell for a traditional Catholic funeral. A long line of cars followed the hearse to the Edison Cemetery on the outskirts of town, where he was buried. Over his name on the flat headstone is the nickname that he always used when signing letters to friends: "Ti Jean" (for little Jack).

The gravesite of Jack Kerouac, "king of the beats," and his wife, Stella, at Edison Cemetery in Lowell.

Amesbury

Union Cemetery
Haverhill Road (Route 110)

John Greenleaf Whittier
1807–1892

On Friday, September 9, 1892, the featured article occupying the entire front page of *The Amesbury News* declared, "The hour has come! and America's beloved poet has passed within the Eternal Gate!" Elaborate ceremonies were held in Amesbury for their "leading citizen" and "the people's poet," John Greenleaf Whittier. The opera house in Amesbury was filled to capacity, as many distinguished people from far and wide attended his memorial service or sent special messages to be read.

Although Whittier, a Quaker, is chiefly remembered for his idyllic poems imbued with the flavor of New England life, such as "The Barefoot Boy" and "Snowbound," he was also well known in his day as a staunch abolitionist. He wrote and edited for several influential abolitionist journals, and much of his poetry reflected his political views. The farmhouse where he was born in nearby Haverhill is open to the public, as is the home where he lived in Amesbury. Several signs point the way to his grave site in Union Cemetery—one atop a high pole proclaims, "Here Lies Whittier."

➻ **Directions to Union Cemetery:** The cemetery is on Route 110, east of the center of town, and the grave site is well marked.

Mount Prospect Cemetery
Elm Street

Al Capp
1909–1979

When cartoonist Al Capp died at the age of 70 in Cambridge, Massachusetts, newspapers around the country carried a poignant cartoon of the Dogpatch characters, Li'l Abner and Daisy Mae, weeping. Capp had been retired for 2 years, but for the previous 43 years he had been the creator of one of the most popular comic strips in the world. A long-running Broadway play and two movies were based on the strip, and such characters as Li'l Abner, Daisy Mae, Moonbeam McSwine, Senator Jack S. Phogbound, and Mammy and Pappy Yocom became household names.

A large, white marble tombstone marks his grave, with the name Alfred Gerald Capp and a quote from Thomas Gray's "Elegy Written in a Country Churchyard": "The plowman homeward plods his weary way, / And leaves the world to darkness and to me."

➤➤ **Directions to Mount Prospect Cemetery:** From Route 95 (north) take the Amesbury exit to Route 110 West (Elm Street), the cemetery is on the left; the grave site is toward the back of the cemetery.

South of Boston

Most of the cemeteries along the South Shore are fairly small, but their significance outstrips their size. The names on the tomb stones found here are sure to evoke memories of your earliest grade school history lessons.

Sharon

Rockridge Cemetery
East Street

Deborah Sampson Gannett
1760–1827

In 1782, Deborah Sampson, a healthy, rugged young woman of 22, donned men's clothing and showed up in Worcester to enlist in the Continental Army under the name of Robert Shurtleff. No documents or physical examination were required, so along with 50 other young recruits she marched off to West Point, where she received a uniform and military equipment.

She took part in several military skirmishes and during one at Tarrytown, New York, she was shot in the thigh. She managed to dress her own wounds, but several months later, while defending the city of Philadelphia, she fell victim to typhoid fever—and this time her true gender was discovered.

She was honorably discharged in 1783 at West Point, but without the usual soldier's pension. Several years later, married and the mother of three children, she was aided by Paul Revere in securing not only a small pension but some back pay as well.

When she died in 1827, her husband (Benjamin Gannett), then ill himself, applied to the government for a widower's pension (the first such request). This time Congress finally recognized Deborah as a fully accredited soldier and war hero, and granted her husband a full pension.

In the summer of 1983, Deborah Sampson Gannett, a.k.a. Robert Shurtleff, was designated by the state House of Representatives as the Official Heroine of the Commonwealth. A large statue of her was commissioned, which stands in front of the Public Library in Sharon, her hometown. Her grave site bears the traditional soldier's flag and the inscription on her stone says "Deborah Sampson Gannett / Robert Shurtleff / The Female Soldier / Service 1781 to 1783."

➼ **Directions to Rockridge Cemetery:** Take Pond Street from the center of Sharon to East Street (left turn); the cemetery is at the intersection of East and Mountain streets. The grave site is on the far east side of the cemetery (near the fence).

Medfield   *Vine Lake Cemetery*
Off Route 27

The town of Medfield is a short distance northwest of Sharon (Route 27) and here, in the old section of the Vine Lake Cemetery, are a number of graves bearing the name of Plimpton. One of the more illustrious members of this large family is James Plimpton (1828–

1911), the inventor of the modern roller skates. Plimpton, the father of three daughters, leased his "guidable parlor skates" in franchised rinks where unchaperoned Victorian women could enjoy this "chaste social activity." By the late 1871 roller skating became a national craze and Plimpton became a wealthy man.

➤➤ **Directions to Vine Lake Cemetery:** Vine Lake Cemetery is off Route 27 in Medfield. The grave site is in the old section of the cemetery.

First Parish Cemetery   **Norwell**
24 River Street

John Cheever
1912–1982

John Cheever, a much-honored writer of novels and short stories chronicling the lives of contemporary suburbanites, is buried in a spot that his readers would well recognize. The cemetery is located in the center of a typical little New England town, across the street from the old First Parish Church, a 17th-century meeting-house. It is on a hilly, shaded plot of land, enclosed by a white picket fence. The quiet streets bordering the cemetery are lined with a few small shops (Cheever's mother once owned and ran one of them) and substantial homes. It is a scene reminiscent of the small towns Cheever liked to write about—St. Botolphs, Shady Hill and Bullet Park.

Although a native of this area, Cheever resided in Ossining, New York, at the time of his death at age 70 from lung cancer. His body was brought back to Norwell for burial in the family plot.

A short Episcopalian service attended by family and close friends was held at the First Parish Church. His friend and colleague, author John Updike, eulogized him by saying, "He was a teller of tales purely, and that purity contributed to the esteem in which he was held."

Following the service his flag-draped coffin (he was a veteran of World War I) was carried to the hearse and driven across the road to the cemetery. Family and friends walked the short distance behind it. The burial site, beneath a large maple tree, is marked by three identical tombstones, those of his parents and his own. His stone, decorated with a small American flag, simply bears his name and dates; beneath the name on his father's stone is the inscription, "We are the stuff as dreams are made of."

➦ **Directions to First Parish Cemetery:** Take Exit 14 from Route 93 and follow signs to Norwell center. The cemetery is easy to locate, as is the stone; enter the small gate from the parking lot and the grave site is to your left, not far from the white picket fence.

Marshfield   *Winslow Burying Ground*
Winslow Cemetery Road

Daniel Webster
1782–1852

Daniel Webster, considered one of the greatest American orators of all times, is well remembered for his famous lines from an impassioned debate to save the Union, "Liberty and Union, now and forever, one and inseparable." Ralph Waldo Emerson said of him at the time of Webster's death, "Nature had not in our days, or not since Napoleon, cut out such a masterpiece."

As the news of his death traveled across the country on October 24, 1852, flags everywhere were lowered to half mast. On the following Friday, the day of his funeral, the post office, schools and all businesses in Boston closed. In Cambridge, lectures at Harvard University ceased for the day. Buildings were draped in black and the Bunker Hill monument, the scene of two of Webster's most famous addresses, was cloaked in mourning as well.

In his will Webster had expressed the wish to be buried "without the least show or ostentation." The family had planned to do so, but they were besieged with requests from those who wished to come and pay

a final tribute to this much-loved and respected man. The open casket was placed on the lawn in front of Webster's home in Marshfield, and thousands of people came to pass by his bier. A private service was held inside the house, and then his casket was taken to the small cemetery nearby.

The gravestone of Daniel Webster in Winslow Burying Ground, Marshfield, bears an inscription written by the orator himself.

The family plot is now set off by an iron railing, and in the center is a modest granite monument. Years earlier, Webster had designed the monument himself and written the lengthy religious inscription to be carved on it.

This cemetery was immortalized in Stephen Vincent Benét's famous short story, "The Devil and Daniel Webster": "And they say that if you go to his grave and speak loud and clear, 'Dan'l Webster—Dan'l Webster!' the ground'll begin to shiver and the trees begin to shake. And after a while you'll hear a deep voice saying, 'Neighbor, how stands the Union?' "

➡ **Directions to Winslow Burying Ground:** From Route 139 in Marshfield center, take 3A south for about 2 miles. Turn east onto Winslow Cemetery Road (well marked). The Webster grave is easily identified.

Duxbury *Miles Standish Burying Ground*
Chestnut Street

The three most famous occupants of this small historic graveyard are those immortalized in Henry Wadsworth Longfellow's classic poem *The Courtship of Miles Standish*—John Alden (c.1599–1687), his wife, Priscilla (1602–c.1682), and the unsuccessful suitor, Miles Standish (c.1584–1656). All three were passengers on the *Mayflower,* and John and Miles were both signers of the Mayflower Compact and leaders in the Pilgrim community.

Miles Standish's grave site is marked by a large boulder with his name carved in bold letters on it and surrounded by a low stone wall, mounted with four cannons. The Aldens' grave markers are typical slate colonial headstones with winged skulls. (The Aldens' house, built in 1653 when the couple moved from Plymouth to Duxbury, has been preserved and is open to the public.)

➼ **Directions to Miles Standish Burying Ground:** In South Duxbury, from the flagpole at Hall's Corner, drive west to Chestnut Street. The small cemetery is on the corner and the grave sites are easily located.

Mayflower Cemetery
Route 3A

Ruth Wakefield
1905–1977

In Mayflower Cemetery on Route 3A in Duxbury is the grave site of the woman who originated chocolate chip cookies. Back in the early 1930s, she and her husband, Ken, ran the Toll House Inn in Whitman, Massachusetts, and it was well known for its fine food. While baking cookies one morning, Ruth was running a little late, so instead of taking time to melt the chocolate, she chopped up bits of chocolate pieces and tossed them into the batter. She hoped they would melt as the cookies baked. The cookies turned out chunky and still filled with the chocolate bits, but one bite told Ruth she was on to something new. Sure enough, they were a hit and the restaurant became famous for them. (Unfortunately, the Toll House Inn burned to the ground in 1984.)

➺ **Directions to Mayflower Cemetery:** The cemetery is south of the Town Hall on Route 3A; turn right after you enter the main gate (Linden Avenue) and then the third left (Cypress Avenue); the grave is on the left.

Plymouth

Burial Hill
Summer and Market Streets

Burial Hill was known as Fort Hill until 1698, and it was here where the Pilgrims built their fort, which also served as their first meetinghouse. A long flight of stone steps leads up to this site, which offers a spectacular, panoramic view of the harbor. It is easy to see why the Pilgrims chose this as their first defensive position.

This site is also believed to be where the Pilgrims buried their dead—those who died in that first hard winter—in unmarked graves. Most of the first settlers who survived were buried in new settlements that became the surrounding towns. Monuments to the Founding Fathers who were undoubtedly buried here were later erected on this site. Among those so honored is William Bradford (1590–1657), who shortly after arriving in Plymouth was elected governor of Plymouth Colony, following the untimely death of John Carver, the first governor. So strong and reliable was Bradford's leadership that he was returned to office 30 times for one-year terms. A tall memorial is inscribed with the words "Under this stone rest the ashes of William Bradford / a zealous puritan and sincere Christian / Gov. of Ply. Col. from April 1621 to 1657, / (the year he died aged 69) / except 5 yrs. which he declined."

➺ **Directions to Burial Hill:** Located in the center of town behind the First Church; steps leading up the hill are on the south side.

Fall River   *Oak Grove Cemetery*
765 Prospect Street

Lizzie Borden
1860–1927

Lizzie Borden does not rest in peace. Ever since she was accused of the ax-murder of her father and step-mother in 1892, songs, poems, books, plays, movies and television specials continue to be written about her. Criminal investigators, both amateur and professional, still pore over her trial records, and in 1992, a pathologist, on the strength of "new scientific evidence," petitioned the courts to have the bodies of her parents exhumed. The guilt or innocence of Lizzie has yet to be satisfactorily proven.

Lizzie died shortly before her 67th birthday, having never fully recovered from surgery a year before. (Her sister, Emma, living in New Hampshire, died ten days later from injuries received in a fall.) A private funeral service was held for Lizzie at Maplecroft, the fashionable house she had purchased after her acquittal, and was attended by a few friends and relatives. She left an estate valued at more than $1 million, and her largest gift of money went to the Animal Rescue League of Fall River. "I have been fond of animals," she wrote in her will, "and their need is great and there are so few who care for them."

Her small headstone in the family plot reads "Lizbeth," the name she had chosen for herself after her trial. Her sister, Emma, is buried next to her.

Also buried in Oak Grove Cemetery is Cornelia Otis Skinner (1901–1979), author and actress, and William T. Grant (1876–1972) whose chain of small, inexpensive department stores were popular throughout the Northeast for many years. (Some are still operating.)

➺ **Directions to Oak Grove Cemetery:** A map is available at Fall River Historical Society, 451 Rock Street, which houses a collection of Borden memorabilia. The cemetery is at the end of Prospect Street; go to the left of the monument as you enter, and then take the next left. The Borden-Almy lot is on the left. The Grant and Skinner grave sites are along one of the main roads.

Cape Cod and the Islands

The beauty and tranquility of Cape Cod and the islands have long made this area a haven for poets, writers and artists of every creative expression. Many of them made their home on the islands and many chose to be buried here. But the area has also produced celebrities of its own, particularly those whose life's work has been involved with the sea. The small seaside cemeteries of Cape Cod and the islands attest to the highly individualistic character of its inhabitants—both old and new.

Oak Grove Cemetery **Falmouth**
Jones Road

Katherine Lee Bates
1859–1929

A native daughter of Cape Cod, Katherine Lee Bates was born on Main Street in Falmouth. She graduated from Wellesley College in 1880 and became a professor of English literature, serving in that position for 34 years. While there she wrote several books of poetry, children's books and many scholarly works, but she is best remembered for her poem (later set to music) "America the Beautiful."

She died in Wellesley and her ashes were returned to Falmouth to be buried in the family plot. Under her name and dates on her tombstone is the inscription "America, America, God shed His grace on thee." The town has placed a bench beside the stone for the hundreds of visitors who come here each year to view it.

➤➤ **Directions to Oak Grove Cemetery:** Gifford Street is off Main Street (across from the fire station). Turn west at the first light onto Jones Road and the cemetery is a short distance. The stone is in the northeast corner of the cemetery.

Woods Hole

Church of the Messiah Cemetery
22 Church Street

All summer long the tiny harbor area of Woods Hole is jammed with cars lining up for the ferries to Martha's Vineyard and Nantucket. But many of those who live in Woods Hole are closely involved with the scientific community that flourishes here. This is where the internationally known science centers for oceanographic research and marine biology studies are located. As such, scientists from around the world have visited the southwest tip of Cape Cod, and many have stayed on to continue their work here.

Many noted scientists and doctors who have made important contributions to the scientific world are buried in the small cemetery of the Church of the Messiah. Among them: Frank R. Lillie (1870–1947), former director of the Woods Hole Oceanographic Institute and president of the Woods Hole Biological Laboratory, who is credited with shaping both institutions; Selman A. Waksman (1888–1973), who won a Nobel Prize in 1952 for the discovery of streptomycin and its value in treating tuberculosis (he also coined the term *antibiotic*); and David Hume (1917–1973) an early pioneer in kidney transplants.

➡ **Directions to Church of the Messiah Cemetery:** Church Street is west off Route 28 south, just before entering the village of Woods Hole. The small cemetery is directly behind the church and the stones are easy to find.

Barnstable

The old "King's Highway," more commonly known as Route 6A to tourists, travels through the most historic part of Cape Cod. Along the way it passes through the center of small villages where you will see clusters of old slate headstones enclosed behind a low stone wall, denoting the village cemetery. One such burial ground along the road in Barnstable has a memorial to one of its most distinguished former citizens encased within the stone wall. The large granite memorial stone has been inscribed with the words "In this cemetery lie / the mortal remains / of / Capt. John Percival / known as 'Mad Jack' / Born Apr. 3, 1779 / Died Sept. 17, 1862 / in command of / 'Old Ironsides' / on 52,279 mile voyage / around the world / 1844–1846."

Centerville

St. Francis Xavier Cemetery
Pine Street

Joseph E. Cronin
1906–1984

He was known to his many friends from Fenway Park to Cape Cod as "Joe" and is considered by most to be one of the all-time Major League shortstop greats. When he signed on with the Red Sox in 1934, Cronin was paid a quarter of a million dollars, the highest salary ever paid to a baseball player at that time. During his term as general manager of the Red Sox, he was elected to the Baseball Hall of Fame (1956), and from 1959 until 1973 he was president of the American League.

He died in his home on the Cape at the age of 77, after a long battle with cancer, and many of his baseball friends attended a funeral mass at St. Francis Xavier Church in Hyannis.

➤➤ **Directions to St. Francis Xavier Cemetery:** Pine Street runs north from the "four corners" (center) of Centerville. The cemetery is well marked on the east side of the road and the grave site is toward the northwest corner.

Chatham

Seaside Cemetery
Route 28

Bobby Hackett
1915–1976

Bobby Hackett, known for his melodic jazz improvisations during the Big Band era, played many instru-

The gravestone of jazz musician Bobby Hackett at Seaside Cemetery, Chatham, depicts his favorite instrument, the cornet.

ments, but the cornet was his specialty. His handsome tombstone in Seaside Cemetery in Chatham is engraved with a picture of his famous cornet. Hackett played with most of the top bands during the Big Band era, and he is best remembered by jazz lovers for his solo with the Glen Miller Band, playing "String of Pearls."

➤➤ **Directions to Seaside Cemetery:** The cemetery is just before the center of Chatham, on the west side of Route 28. The grave site is in the northwest section.

Provincetown

Provincetown Cemetery
Cemetery Road

Rear Admiral Donald B. MacMillan
1874–1970

Rear Admiral MacMillian, the son of a Provincetown fisherman who was lost at sea, was affectionately known to his thousands of friends and admirers as "Captain Mac." He died at the age of 95 in Provincetown, the last survivor of the Peary Expediton that discovered the North Pole. He made 30 trips to the Arctic in his two-masted schooner, the *Bowdoin,* in uncharted waters, and made valuable contributions to geological history. Concerned for the health of the Eskimos, on one of his trips he carried 2,000 toothbrushes to distribute to Eskimo children.

When he retired in 1960, his schooner was sent to Mystic Seaport Museum in Connecticut. One of the main fishing piers in Provincetown is named in his honor, and an exhibit of his explorations is on view in the Provincetown Museum at the Pilgrim Monument.

➼ **Directions to Provincetown Cemetery:** From Route 6, turn west onto Cornwell Street at the traffic light; the first road on the left is Cemetery Street. Turn in the second entrance to the cemetery (the main road). The MacMillan plot is on the left, toward the end of the road.

Chilmark, Martha's Vineyard

Abel's Hill Cemetery
South Road

Chilmark is one of the more sparsely populated sections of Martha's Vineyard, offering a perfect hideaway for celebrities who come here to get away from it all. Many headstones in the old cemetery on Abel's Hill (named for an Indian whose wigwam once stood on this spot) bear witness to the number of people, popular in the arts, who chose this as their final resting place. Two such stones with well-worn paths leading up to them indicate the grave sites of John Belushi and Lillian Hellman.

John Belushi
(1949–1982)

During the late 1970s, John Belushi was one of the best known, most talented comedians in television, due to his work on the program "Saturday Night Live." He died in California at the age of 33 from an accidental drug overdose. Just three years before he died he had

This massive, engraved rock marks the burial site of comedian John Belushi at Abel's Hill Cemetery on Martha's Vineyard.

purchased a home in Chilmark, and according to his manager, "it was the only place where he said he slept well."

A private service for about 200 invited guests and relatives was held at the First Congregational Church in West Tisbury. The procession from the church to the cemetery, about 2 miles away, was led by Belushi's long-time friend, comedian Dan Aykroyd, who was dressed in black and rode on a Harley-Davidson motorcycle. During the graveside service, which was also private, James Taylor strummed his guitar and sang "That Lonesome Road."

Belushi's grave, near the entrance to the cemetery, is marked by a large, sprawling rock with his last name emblazed on it in bold, dark letters. The ground around the rock is well worn by visitors. Small piles of beach pebbles and seashells are often found around the memorial (a custom in many Cape Cod cemeteries).

Lillian Hellman
1905–1984

When Lillian Hellman, author, playwright and motion-picture scenarist, died on Martha's Vineyard in 1984, many prominent figures in the entertainment world came from miles away to pay their last respects. Her closest friends were already on the island—friends and neighbors who lived there. At her graveside many of them—William Styron, Jules Feiffer, Patricia Neal, Robert Brustein, John Hersey and Jerome Wiesner (president of the Massachusetts Institute of Technology, where Hellman often lectured)—paid special tribute to her in their eulogies.

Hellman's burial plot in the exclusive cemetery was provided for her by Wiesner, and the gravestone was placed there by Hersey. It is a small piece of blue-gray slate with her name and dates written on it and a long writer's quill etched beneath it. Like other well-visited graves, it is often surrounded with colored beach pebbles and seashells.

➤➤ **Directions to Abel's Hill Cemetery:** The cemetery is located on the west side of South Road, near Chilmark Pond. Belushi's grave is just as you enter the cemetery, and Hellman's is farther back on the far right side.

Two other popular figures of the entertainment world who are buried on Martha's Vineyard are stage actress Katherine Cornell (1893–1974) in the Village Cemetery in Vineyard Haven and Ruth Gordon (1896–1985) in Edgartown Cemetery, Edgartown.

Prospect Hill Cemetery   **Nantucket**
Milk Street Extension

Maria Mitchell
1818–1889

Maria Mitchell, Nantucket's favorite daughter, was America's first female astronomer. She won an international reputation in 1847 when she discovered a new comet and received a gold medal from the king of Denmark for doing so. In 1848, she became the first woman fellow of the American Academy of Arts and Sciences. In 1861, she was appointed professor of astronomy and director of the observatory at the newly founded Vassar College, where she remained until her death in 1880.

Maria Mitchell's home and observatory are now part of the Maria Mitchell Association, which also includes a science library, a museum of natural science and an aquarium.

➤➤ **Directions to Prospect Hill Cemetery:** From Main Street walk west to the monument and turn left onto Milk Street. The Maria Mitchell Association is on the right (house and observatory on Vestal Street) and the cemetery is farther down Milk Street, on the left. The Mitchell family plot is just inside the cemetery and easy to identify.

Central Massachusetts

This area is called the state's "heartland," and it has produced a bumber crop of strong-minded, self-reliant individuals who have left their mark on the world. Proud monuments mark the graves of such diverse citizens as the founder of the American Red Cross, the inventor of the liquid fuel rocket, the first postman, and the doctor who gave us "The Pill."

Oxford *North Oxford Cemetery*
Route 12

Clara Barton
1821–1912

When Clara Barton, the "Angel of the Battlefield," died of pneumonia at the age of 91, *The New York Sun* eulogized her by saying in part, "Clara Barton was more than brave. She devoted her life to humanity. . . . Is it not the finest kind of glory that when the American Red Cross is seen or mentioned the name of Clara Barton comes to the mind like a benediction?"

Working in Washington, D.C., as a clerk during the Civil War, Barton was appalled by the suffering of the wounded Union soldiers following the Battle of Bull Run. She went among the wounded offering help where she could and then organized an extensive food and clothing drive to take care of their needs. It was the beginning of her lifelong work, not only as the founder of the American Red Cross but to further the cause of the International Red Cross as well. It was through her efforts that the Red Cross became involved with natural disaster relief.

She was born and raised in the small rural town of North Oxford, and her home (open for tours) and farm are now operated as a summer camp for diabetic children. Her grave site in nearby Oxford center is marked by a tall granite cross topped with red granite. The inscription notes her participation in three wars: the Civil War, the Franco-Prussian War and the Spanish-American War (when she rode a mule wagon at the age of 77 to nurse the wounded).

➺ **Directions to North Oxford Cemetery:** From Route 90 (Massachusetts Turnpike) take the Route 12 exit to Oxford center. The cemetery is on the west side of the road and the grave site is to the right as you enter.

Hope Cemetery **Worcester**
Webster Street

Robert H. Goddard
1882–1945

Robert Goddard, the "Father of Modern Rocketry," had to miss a lot of school as a young boy due to a liver ailment. He spent his idle hours reading the books of H. G. Wells and fantasizing about futuristic rocket inventions. Using empty coffee cans and almost anything he could get his hands on, he began to do some scientific experimenting in his own backyard, often to the consternation of his neighbors.

He later went on to a technical school and taught physics at Clark University, but he never gave up his experiments. In 1926 he launched the first liquid fuel rocket from a neighbor's farm in Auburn, Massachusetts. Goddard went on to complete many more experiments—helping to usher in both the space age and the long-range arms race.

Goddard died at the age of 63 in Baltimore, Maryland, and his body was returned to Worcester for burial at Hope Cemetery. There are several memorials to him in Worcester: one at Goddard Park (a replica of a rocket), an exhibit at Clark University's Goddard Library (containing memorabilia of his early rocketry experiments) and a plaque on the grounds of the Pakachoag Golf Course—the actual 1926 launch site.

➤➤ **Directions to Hope Cemetery:** From Route 290 take the Hope Avenue exit; go to the end of Hope Avenue.

Shrewsbury

Shrewsbury is the quintessential little New England town that grew up along the famous "Old" Boston Post Road in central Massachusetts. This was the original Boston Post Road (there are two others), being so designated in 1673. It is said that at the height of stagecoach travel more than 2,000 coaches a week traveled this road. Many of the old inns where the stagecoach stopped en route from Boston to New York are still in existence (one of the best known is the Wayside Inn in Sudbury). But here in Shrewsbury lived the man who probably did more than any other person to promote stagecoach travel and was, in fact, the first mailman: Levi Pease.

Mountain View Cemetery
Main and Boylston Streets

Captain Levi Pease
1739–1824

Captain Levi Pease was a blacksmith by trade and a dispatch rider in his spare time, and was also known as a shrewd trader. During the Revolutionary War he was commissioned to purchase horses and supplies for Washington's army. In 1783, after purchasing an inn and stagecoach stop on the Old Post Road in Shewsbury, he established a stagecoach line between Boston and Hartford. He advertised an on-time departure schedule for his coaches, a risky and expensive way of doing business at that time, since most stagecoaches could not afford to leave for a destination until the coach was full. Pease lost money at first, but his coaches were always on time, and reliability finally paid off. He was granted the first contract with the U.S. government for carrying the mail.

A bronze plaque embedded in a large boulder in Mountain View Cemetery in Shrewsbury chronicles the achievements of Captain Levi Pease as a soldier, a government forager, a dispatch bearer, the organizer and proprietor of the first stagecoach lines in the United States and the first contractor for carrying the U.S. mail.

Mountain View Cemetery was established in 1730 as the town "burying place" and has been used as such for many generations. Still in use, it has a newer section toward the back, and buried there is a man of the 20th century who lays claim to significant achievements of quite another type. Dr. Gregory G. Pincus (1903–1967) won many awards for his research and development during his lifetime, but nothing brought him such worldwide acclaim as a pill called "Enovid." Known to a whole new generation as "The Pill," the first successful oral contraceptive, it became the major method of birth control used throughout the world. The inscription on his tombstone reads "A Great and Kindly Man."

➤➤ **Directions to Mountain View Cemetery:** Located in the center of Shrewsbury, behind the Congregational Church. The Pease grave site is just inside the stone gates and the Pincus grave site is toward the back in the new section.

Evergreen Cemetery   **Leominster**
North Main Street (Route 13)

Joseph Palmer
1794–1873

While Joseph Palmer may not rank as a notable New Englander, his tombstone in Evergreen Cemetery has brought him enduring fame and thus qualifies him for inclusion in this book. No one can pass the tombstone without taking a second glance and reading the inscription. Carved into the sizable monument is the face of a man with a long fluffy beard. Under the face is the inscription: "Persecuted for wearing the beard."

In 1830 men did not wear beards, and when Joseph Palmer, a strong individualist and a freethinker, decided to grow one, his neighbors attacked him with taunts and threats. Not one to bend to such censure, Palmer just let his beard grow longer and fuller. On one occasion, however, a gang of men, with soap and razor in hand, chased after him with the intention of shaving off his beard. Palmer was able to fight them off, but the local police arrived and threw him in jail for inciting to

Joseph Palmer's unusual monument at Evergreen Cemetery in Leominster declares that he was "persecuted for wearing the beard."

riot! He refused to pay the fine and remained in jail for some time.

Palmer later left the area and joined the utopian community Fruitlands, in Harvard, Massachusetts, founded by Bronson Alcott. There he was perfectly free to walk about in peace with his beard intact.

➼ **Directions to Evergreen Cemetery:** On North Main Street (Route 12) just south of Route 2.

Western Massachusetts

Both the Old Mohawk Trail and the modern Massachusetts Turnpike wind their way through this scenic part of the state. Rolling countryside, snowcapped mountain peaks and panoramic vistas have always made this area a favorite destination for artists, musicians and craftspeople. Herman Melville, Edith Wharton, Emily Dickinson, Nathaniel Hawthorne, Serge Koussevitzky and Norman Rockwell are just a few who have found inspiration here.

Springfield

The industrial city of Springfield is the metropolis of the western part of the state, and over the years, companies that manufacture everything from toys to guns have flourished here. A walk through the beautifully landscaped Springfield Cemetery, where 14 generations of townspeople have been buried, is a lesson in the history of this city. Civic pride is well evident in the many interesting memorials found here, most particularly (and often photographed), the 6-foot-high monument of a two-story dwelling commissioned in 1896 for Andrew Titus, a successful Victorian real estate man who is buried here. Two gentlemen who have endeared themselves to the hearts of young children are also buried here: Milton Bradley and Thornton Burgess.

Springfield Cemetery
171 Maple Street

Milton Bradley
(1836–1911)

Milton Bradley established a lithography business in Springfield in 1860, but business was not going well and he soon became depressed. A friend, trying to cheer him up one evening, suggested they play an old English board game. It cheered him up so much that he decided to make one of his own. He called it "The Checkered Game of Life," and it proved to be so popular with friends and family that he was soon keeping his printers busy all day long reproducing it.

In 1864, along with two partners, he launched Milton Bradley Company, and to this day, the name is almost synonymous with games and toys. Bradley, an early advocate of Friedrich Froebel, the German educator and founder of the kindergarten system, insisted his games and toys always have an educational purpose. He was a pioneer in the manufacture of educational materials, publishing the first book in the United States on kindergartens.

Thornton Burgess
1874–1965

Thornton Burgess was the favorite bedtime storyteller to millions of children during the 1940s and 1950s. It was once noted at that time that if the children of America could elect a candidate for president of the United States, it would most likely be Thornton Burgess.

Burgess was born in Sandwich on Cape Cod but moved to Springfield in the early 1900s to become editor of a local publishing company. He began writing bedtime stories for his young son, based on his childhood memories of the woods he had roamed as a child in Sandwich. Thus was born a cast of characters such as Peter Cottontail, Reddy Fox, Bobby Coon and Mother West Wind and her bag of Merry Little Breezes, and locales such as Gully Lane, Green Meadows and the Briar Patch that delighted children everywhere.

What made Burgess's stories unique was his love of nature and his concern for the environment which in turn, inspired young people toward conservation. His stories have been credited by many conservationists with helping to bring about much-needed legislation for the preservation of wildlife and natural beauty.

When he retired in 1960, at the age of 86, he had written 15,000 stories for children and some 70 books that sold 7.5 million copies. He died at the age of 91; his only son, Thornton W. Burgess III, had died the previous year. The Thornton Burgess Society in Sandwich, Massachusetts, keeps his memory very much alive with a museum, a book and gift shop and the Green Briar Nature Center, where you can still walk the Old Briar Patch Trail.

➻ **Directions to Springfield Cemetery:** The cemetery is on the south side of Springfield (toward the Connecticut River); take State Street south to Maple Street. The office has a map of the cemetery; the Burgess stone is on Monument Avenue the Bradley stone is near Laurel Avenue.

Amherst

West Cemetery
Triangle Street

Emily Dickinson
1830–1886

Emily Dickinson, one of America's great poets, spent most of her life as a recluse in her family's Victorian house in Amherst. She viewed life from the curtained window of her second-floor bedroom, where she prolifically composed some of the most astonishing poems and then hid them away in a bureau drawer. She died at the age of 55 from Bright's disease; her body, dressed in white, was placed in a white casket "with violets and ground pine over it." Following a simple service with only family and a few friends in attendance, her casket was carried through the woods and meadows to the graveyard nearby.

After Emily's death, her sister Vinnie found the poems and proceeded to have them published. Until that time only 7 of her poems had appeared in print, but over the succeeding years, from 1890 until 1945, about 1,775 poems, along with her voluminous correspondence, were published.

She is buried in the family burial plot, which is completely surrounded by a wrought-iron fence. The inscription on her white tombstone says simply "Called Back."

➤➤ **Directions to West Cemetery:** The Emily Dickinson House (mostly the author's bedroom) at 280 Main Street is open for special tours during the summer. The cemetery is just around the corner (south) on Triangle Street.

Stockbridge

Stockbridge Cemetery
Main and Church Streets

Elizabeth Freeman
c.1744–1829

This old cemetery contains the graves of both the early settlers to Stockbridge and the native Americans who preceded them. It is an interesting place for reading epitaphs. Toward the rear of the cemetery in the prominent Sedgwick family plot is the tombstone of Elizabeth Freeman, better known as "Mum Bet."

As a young African-American servant in the home of Colonel John Ashley, where the Sheffield Declaration of Independence was drawn up, Mum Bet became aware of her rights of being "born free and equal." She sought the help of a neighbor, Theodore Sedgwick (congressman and senator), who argued her case and won her freedom. Mum Bet then went to work for the Sedgwicks as a free woman and became a much-loved member of their family.

Her epitaph, written by Sedgwick's daughter, Catharine Maria Sedgwick, tells her story: "Her supposed age was 85 years. She was born a slave and remained a slave for nearly thirty years. She could neither read nor write yet in her own sphere she had no superior nor equal. She nether wasted time nor property. She never violated a trust nor failed to perform a duty. In every situation of domestic trial she was the most efficient helper, and the tenderest friend. Good Mother, farewell."

Norman Rockwell
1894–1978

Norman Rockwell always insisted that he was not an artist. "I am an illustrator, a storyteller," he once told an interviewer. "Painting and illustration are two separate fields, like opera and popular music." His illustrations, however, of which more than 4,000 are on view at various times in the Norman Rockwell Museum in Stockbridge, can still evoke tremendous emotion.

He sold his first illustration to the *Saturday Evening Post* when he was 22 years old and subsequently painted 360 covers for the magazine. His illustrations catch the joys and sorrows of life's simplest adventures, always striking a universal chord among his viewers. Some of his most famous covers are those involving children, such as one of a grandmother and her young grandson saying grace before lunch in a rundown railroad station restaurant. Another shows a little African-American girl being escorted to school in the company of four U.S. Deputy Marshals. His "Four Freedoms," depicting the

The gravestone of the beloved illustrator Norman Rockwell at Stockbridge Cemetery in Stockbridge.

freedoms of a democratic society and painted during World War II, are considered among his most important works. During the war years they traveled all over the country as part of a special exhibition and raised more than $130 million in aid.

His funeral service was held at St. Paul's Episcopal Church, and burial was in the town cemetery on Main Street (a street he immortalized in another of his best-remembered illustrations). A large plain polished granite stone with the name "Rockwell" on it, surrounded by low bushes, marks his grave site.

➤➤ **Directions to Stockbridge Cemetery:** The cemetery is on the corner of Main and Church streets, across from the town hall. The Sedgwick family plot is at the end of the central driveway. The Rockwell plot is toward the back in the northeast.

Lenox *Church on the Hill Cemetery*
Main and Greenwood Streets

Serge Koussevitzky
1874–1951

Russsian-born Serge Koussevitzky was the conductor of the Boston Symphony Orchestra from 1924 to 1949, and under his direction it became one of the finest in the nation. He established the Tanglewood summer concerts and the Tanglewood Music Center in Lenox, which draws thousands of music lovers and students to this area every summer. About 20 percent of the members of America's major orchestras count themselves among the Tanglewood alumni, attesting to the significance of the music education received here.

More than 1,000 people attended Koussevitzky funeral service in the Episcopal Church of the Advent in Boston. As the service began, 76 strokes of the church bell, one for each year of his life, were tolled. The service was conducted in both Anglican and Russian concepts. A total of 14 players of string instruments from the Boston Symphony Orchestra played special pieces, and songs were sung by a Russian choir of five men. The 20 honorary pallbearers included pupils and musical associates of Koussevitzky.

A brief service was held in the Church on the Hill in Lenox the next day, followed by his burial in the hillside cemetery only a few miles from Tanglewood. A small headstone marks his grave site, but just below it, built into the steep hillside, is another memorial to him, a large polished marble stone with the words, "In loving memory of Serge Koussevitzky by the members of The Israel Symphony Orchestra to whom he was a great and inspired leader and a loved and honored friend."

➡ **Directions to Church on the Hill Cemetery:** The cemetery is behind the Church on the Hill in the center of Lenox; the grave site is in the far east corner.

RHODE ISLAND

The ornate grave site of millionaire August Belmont, Island Cemetery, Newport.

Providence Area

The Blackstone River Valley stretches north of Providence, and this little known section of the small state of Rhode Island is well worth discovering. Hearty pioneers carved pasture land from thick forests that once covered the area, and by the late 18th century, there were mill towns along the Blackstone River. This valley is, in fact, the birthplace of America's Industrial Revolution, which began at the Slater Mill in Pawtucket (an Indian name meaning "the place by the waterfall") in 1793.

Providence

The capital city of Rhode Island was founded in 1636 by Roger Williams who had been exiled from Massachusetts for civil and religious nonconformity. He named the new settlement Providence in gratitude "for God's merciful providence unto me in my distress." In the early days of Providence, most families had private burial plots on their own property. But as the city developed and new streets were created, often cutting through the old family burial plots, the graves were moved to a newly established public burying ground (North Burial Ground).

Prospect Terrace
Congdon at Cushing Street

Roger Williams
c.1603–1683

The most impressive grave site in all of Rhode Island, and rightly so, is that of its founder, Roger Williams, who was also called the "founder of religious liberty." An enormous statue of Williams, erected in 1939, stands at the highest point in Providence with a commanding view of the city's skyline. It is surrounded by a small park with flowering trees and shrubs, pathways and benches.

This is not, however, the site where Williams was first buried. Years of research disclosed that he was buried in a spot close to his home (now the rear yard of the famous Sullivan Dorr mansion at the northeast corner of Benefit and Bowen streets); a circular piece of granite marks the spot. A scientific dig of the site in 1860 to uncover the remains of Williams and his wife revealed an interesting surprise. Because the grave site was close to an apple orchard, the roots from one of the apple trees had consumed, over many years, everything organic in their path. What the grave held, besides some nails, bits of decayed wood and a lock of braided hair (presumably that of Mrs. Williams) were the roots of the old apple tree in the shape of a human. Many stories and lectures have circulated about this phenomenon including one small book titled *Who Ate Roger Williams?* written by a chemistry teacher. For many years the roots were on display at the Rhode Island Historical Society in Providence.

The other "remains" of Roger Williams—the rusty, flat-headed nails with decayed wood attached and his wife's braided hair—are contained in a small bronze casket that was placed within the stone base of the statue that now overlooks the city of Providence.

➻ **Directions to Prospect Terrace:** Prospect Terrace can be reached from Benefit Street (the heart of the historic area), turning east onto Meeting Street, and south onto Congdon Street (very hilly area).

North Burial Ground
North Main Street and Branch Avenue

This is the oldest public cemetery in Providence and it was established in 1700 for "a training field, burying ground, and other public uses." Stephen Hopkins (1707–1785), one of the state's most distinguished citizens is buried here, and his grave site is prominently marked. He was ten times governor of the colony of Rhode Island, chief justice of the Superior Court and a signer of the Declaration of Independence. "My hand trembles, but my heart does not," he said as he inscribed his name on the famous document.

Many other prominent Rhode Islanders are buried in this old, rambling cemetery and some of them are noted below.

Horace Mann
1796–1859

A tall, slim granite obelisk, dwarfing the surrounding gravestones, marks the grave of the "Father of American Public Education," Horace Mann. Although more often associated with Boston, Massachusetts, where he instituted the first public school system, or Yellow Springs, Ohio, where he was the founder and president of the innovative Antioch College, he chose to be buried in Providence next to the grave of his first wife, Charlotte. (His second wife, Mary Peabody, was buried here in 1887.)

As Mann lay dying in his home on the campus of Antioch on a warm August evening, his students, upon hearing the news, hurried to his home and quietly filed into his room. One by one they were summoned to his bedside to receive Mann's last words of encouragement and a final handshake. When this was done, he asked them to sing a hymn, which they did, and his final words were, "Now I bid you all good-night."

The next day, the students once again gathered at the Mann home, this time to form a procession escorting Mann's casket to a temporary burial place on the campus. Just the month before, Mann had delivered his last commencement address and in it advised his students: "Be ashamed to die until you have won some victory for humanity."

Annie Smith Peck
1850–1935

Annie Smith Peck, a lecturer on Greek and Roman archaeology, began mountain climbing in 1885 when she was 35 years old. Three years later, attired in knickerbockers, hip-length tunic, stout boots, woolen hose and a soft felt hat tied with a veil, she successfully scaled the Matterhorn, gaining instant fame—as well as much publicity.

Peck's major triumph in mountaineering, however, lay in reaching the summit of the north peak of Huascaran in Peru in 1908. At 21,812 feet (1,500 feet higher than Mount McKinley), it was the highest point yet attained by any American. The peak was later named in Peck's honor.

As an active suffragist, believing women could do anything men could do, Peck took great pride in her accomplishments as a woman. She was the first to climb Mount Coropuna (21,250 feet) in Peru, and upon arriving at the summit, she planted a "Votes for Women" pennant there. She continued her climbing, and at the time of her death in 1935, Peck had climbed all of the tallest mountain peaks in Central and South America, winning many honors and awards. At the age of 82, she climbed her last mountain (Mount Madison in New Hampshire) and then began a world tour. Upon her return, Peck died quietly in New York of bronchial pneumonia. After cremation her ashes were returned to her home state of Rhode Island where she was buried. Her large slab stone bears the inscription, "You have brought uncommon glory to women of all time."

Sarah Helen Whitman
1803–1878

Recalling her tempestuous courtship with Edgar Allan Poe, Sarah Helen Whitman was to write, "He hailed me as an angel sent from heaven to save him from perdition, and clung to my dress so frantically as to tear away a piece of muslin that I wore." An accomplished poet in her own right, she had gotten Poe's attention by writing an anonymous Valentine poem to him in the *New York Home Journal.* He became instantly smitten and in return wrote the poem "To Helen" in her honor.

Their few brief meetings in Providence where she lived (rendezvousing at least once in a graveyard) culminated in their becoming engaged. Sarah agreed to marry Poe on the condition he quit drinking. He didn't, so she broke their engagement within a month. Later, however, she became one of his staunchest defenders, and one of her most acclaimed works is a scholarly brochure titled *Edgar Poe and His Critics.*

Defying conventions of the day, Whitman declared that her motto was "Break all bonds." She left exacting instructions in her will that only a few intimate friends be invited to her funeral and forbade any public announcement of her death until after her interment. She was buried in the family plot with a small square stone with her name on it marking her grave.

Other grave sites of notable men and women in this cemetery are those of various members of the Brown family, particularly Nicholas Brown (1769–1841), an early manufacturer and philanthropist for whom Brown University is named; his brother, Moses Brown (1738–1836), who donated his land for the school that bears the family name, and John Carter Brown (1797–1874), whose remarkable collection of more than 5,600 volumes became the basis of the university's library.

Nearby, another large family plot is that of the Herreshoffs, famous for their shipbuilding. John Brown Herreshoff (1841–1915), totally blind from the time he was 15, began his own sailboat building company in 1856. He was later joined by his brother, Nathaniel Green Herreshoff (1848–1938). Together they went on to design new and radical features for sailboats, and subsequently produced five successful defenders of the America's Cup.

One other grave site worth noting here is that of Charles Henry Dow. Tall weeds almost cover the plain, unadorned headstone of the co-founder of Dow-Jones & Company and founder of the prestigious *Wall Street Journal.*

➡ **Directions to North Burial Ground:** The cemetery is on the north side of Providence, at the intersection of North Main Street and Branch Avenue. A map is available at the office. Dow is at the end of Main Avenue at Magnolia Street, on the right. Hopkins is off Central Avenue at Hopkins Avenue. Herreshoff and Peck are close to Hopkins. Brown and Whitman are on Eastern Avenue and Mann is on Cypress Avenue (very visible).

Swan Point Cemetery
585 Blackstone Boulevard

Swan Point is one of the most beautiful garden cemeteries in New England. Situated on the banks of the

Seekonk River on the outskirts of Providence, lined with carefully pruned flowering trees and shrubs, plus rolling green lawns, it is inhabited almost equally by the living as well as the dead. Along the flower-strewn paths, joggers, walkers, bicyclists and bird-watchers abound. So popular is bird-watching here, that a book called *The Birds of Swan Point* was commissioned and written in 1981 especially for amateur ornithologists.

Swan Point (the name originating from the swan-neck shape of a peninsula jutting into the Seekonk River) is said to be the final resting place of "the movers and shakers of Rhode Island's social, intellectual, artistic and political past." And so it is. On its grounds are interred 23 of the state's governors; Nelson Aldrich (1841–1915), a powerful senator and the grandfather of Nelson Aldrich Rockefeller; George Corliss (1817–1888), the developer of the famous Corliss steam engine; General Ambrose Burnside (1824–1881), a distinguished officer of the Civil War (who also began the fashion of wearing side whiskers, later called "sideburns" in his honor); George Pierce Baker (1866–1935), English professor and dramatist at Harvard and Yale who instituted "campus theater;" and Thomas Wilson Dorr, "the champion of the common man to expand suffrage in Rhode Island" by perpetrating the infamous Dorr's Rebellion.

Thomas Wilson Dorr
1805–1854

Thomas Wilson Dorr was installed in 1842 as the "People's Governor" of Rhode Island in opposition to Samuel King, who had been inaugurated under the colonial charter of 1663, which limited voting rights to landowners. Dorr and his followers staged an ill-fated attack on the Providence armory, which was quickly dispelled. He was captured and charged with high treason and sentenced to solitary confinement at hard labor for life. The conservative government, however, convinced of the strength's of Dorr's cause, drew up a new constitution, greatly liberalizing voting requirements. Following this, the harshness of Dorr's sentence, which was

The "People's Governor," Thomas Dorr, is buried below this stone at Swan Point Cemetery in Providence.

widely condemned, was overturned and one year later, broken in health, he was pardoned and released. Dorr is buried among the "movers and shakers of Rhode Island," and the epitaph on his simple, colonial headstone (adorned with a bronze "governor's marker" and a state flag) reads: "He died in the Faith."

➽ **Directions to Swan Point Cemetery:** The cemetery is on the northeast side of Providence on Blackstone Boulevard. The entrance to the cemetery is marked by a large pile of boulders (dug by hand from the cemetery grounds and drawn by oxen to the site in 1847). The Dorr plot is on the far east side, at a triangle at Forest and Spruce avenues.

Woonsocket

Woonsocket is located on the Blackstone River in the northern part of the state on the Massachusetts border. The rushing waterfalls in the center of the city made it a natural for the founding of the many textile mills that once thrived there. Many of the town's forebears came from Canada to work in the mills, establishing French-speaking schools in the area for their children. One such family that immigrated here from Quebec in 1925 was that of a devout Roman Catholic, Jean-Baptiste Ferron and his wife, Rose de Lima. Their tenth child, Rose, known as "Little Rose of Woonsocket," was to bring everlasting fame to this small, close-knit community.

Precious Blood Cemetery
Route 122

Marie Rose Ferron
1902–1936

Tour buses still trundle through the large open gates leading into Precious Blood Cemetery on the north side of Woonsocket and stop before a large slab stone with the inscription in French: "*Victime de son Jesus*" ("Victim of her Jesus"). This is the grave site of Marie Rose Ferron, a religious young woman, crippled almost from birth with arthritis, who claimed to have visions of Jesus and to exhibit signs of the stigmata (body marks resembling the crucifixion wounds of Jesus). Thousands of people who believed in her mystical phenomena and her ability to cure sickness visited her bedside before she died at the age of 33. However, the Catholic church, after a thorough investigation, found her reported "miracles" invalid and discouraged attempts to canonize her.

When Marie Rose died in 1936, thousands came to her funeral and tearfully watched as the casket was carried into Holy Family Church by six women, dressed in white. At the burial in Precious Blood Cemetery, throngs of those attending rushed the bier and carried off every last flower.

When her father died in 1947, gravediggers "accidentally" opened Marie Rose's coffin and spread the rumor that her body was completely preserved. Once again the throngs gathered at the grave site and hundreds of people, including priests and nuns, stood in the rain to witness the exhumation of "Little Rose." Pathologists who examined the body the next day found it to be well into the advanced stages of decomposition, and she was buried for the last time.

Still, the devout come to visit the grave site. Some say they detect the faint smell of roses about her grave; others take a small pinch of earth to carry away with them as a souvenir.

➤➤ **Directions to Precious Blood Cemetery:** Take route 122 from the center of town, travel north for about 6 miles. As you enter the cemetery gates, follow the road to the right, and the grave site is about halfway down on your left.

Newport Area

Newport, situated on the southern tip of Aquidneck Island between Narragansett Bay and the Atlantic Ocean, was settled in 1639. It is steeped in history as an important colonial seaport and as the site of an outstanding naval academy. But it is probably best known throughout the world as America's most sumptuous summer playground for the very rich during the height of the Gilded Age (c.1870–1898). Today it is one of the most visited tourist sites in New England. Visitors flock here each summer to tour the many magnificent mansions (open to the public) that line Cliff Walk, or to take part in the annual sailing races, boat shows and musical festivals. There are many interesting old cemeteries on the island, including the oldest Jewish cemetery in the country, but the one that best represents Newport is Island Cemetery where millionaires and naval heroes alike are buried.

Newport *Island Cemetery*
Warner Street

Oliver Hazard Perry
1785–1819
Matthew Calbrath Perry
1794–1858

Two of the most outstanding naval heroes in American history are buried in this old, well-maintained cemetery. The brothers Oliver Hazard Perry and Matthew Calbrath Perry had long careers in the navy, both entering the service at the age of 14. Matthew served aboard the flagship of his older brother, Oliver, during the Battle of Lake Erie just after the outbreak of the War of 1812. After forcing the British to surrender, Oliver sent his most celebrated message to his commander, William Henry Harrison, "We have met the enemy and they are ours."

Matthew's naval triumph came when he anchored his four warships in Yedo Bay, Japan, in 1853, demanding to deliver a letter from President Millard Fillmore to the Japanese emperor. This was at a time when Japan was pursuing a policy of total isolation from the West. After six tense days, the emperor finally allowed Perry to present his papers. This resulted in the Treaty of Kanagawa, which opened trade between Japan and the United States.

Oliver Perry was stricken with yellow fever while on a diplomatic mission to South America in 1819. He died aboard his ship off the West Indies at the age of 33. His body was later brought back to Newport where a large monument was erected in his honor. Matthew Perry died at the age of 64 after catching a severe cold that turned to rheumatic gout. He was buried with full military honors in the churchyard at St. Mark's Church in New York City. His body was later returned to Newport to be buried close to other family members.

August Belmont
1853–1924

Upon the death of his father in 1890, August Belmont, then 37 years old, became head of his father's prestigious banking house and heir to the bulk of the Belmont fortune (then estimated at about $25 million). He had been well prepared for this responsibility by his father, and Belmont used his money and influence well. Two of his major accomplishments were the building of the New York subway system and the Cape Cod Canal.

Throughout his remarkable career, August Belmont was one of the most prominent of the America Cup defenders (the races were held in Newport for many years); he gained international fame as breeder of racing horses and built the famous Belmont Park; he also was a pioneer in promoting radio.

The Belmont family had long been prominent leaders in Newport society. August's mother was the daughter of Commodore Matthew C. Perry. Their plot is one of the largest and most elaborate in the cemetery, containing many Perry and Belmont descendants buried side by side. (See photograph, page 64).

Hugh D. Auchincloss, Sr.
1897–1976
Janet Lee Auchincloss
1908–1989

Hugh D. Auchincloss, Sr., was born in Newport at Hammersmith Farm—a home that was to become not only a "summer White House" to President John F. Kennedy but a national shrine as well. Mr. Auchincloss was a very successful lawyer and stockbroker and also worked for a time in both the U.S. Commerce Department and the State Department where he was an aviation specialist.

The Auchincloss family was always a leader in Newport society; however, when Hugh's step-daughter, Jacqueline Lee Bouvier, married Senator John F. Kennedy at St. Mary's Church in Newport in the fall of 1953, the national spotlight was forever turned on his home and his family.

Funeral services were held for the 79-year-old Mr. Auchincloss in both Washington, D.C., and Newport. Janet Auchincloss died 12 years later, in 1989 at the age of 81. She was buried in the Auchincloss family plot in Island Cemetery (although married to Bingham W. Morris).

Mrs. Auchincloss had sold Hammersmith Farm in 1977 to Camelot Gardens, a group of business and professional people that was dedicated to its preservation. It is open throughout the summer months for public tours.

Another grave site of note in this cemetery is that of Richard Morris Hunt (1827–1895), the renowned architect. He designed several of the mansions in Newport, including two of the most sumptuous—The Breakers and Marble House.

➤➤ **Directions to Island Cemetery:** From downtown Newport, go north on Farewell Street, turning east onto Warner Street. Enter the main gate of the cemetery and the Perry monument (tall and prominent) will be halfway back on the west side. The Belmont, Auchincloss and Hunt family plots are on the east side of the cemetery near the chapel.

Common Burying Ground
Farewell Street

Ida Lewis
1842–1911

The land for this cemetery was given to the city of Newport in 1640, originally for strangers, but now contains the remains of many illustrious former citizens. One such grave is that of Newport's beloved female lighthouse keeper, Ida Lewis. For more than 50 years, the keeper of the lighthouse on Lime Rock braved the chilly waters of Newport Harbor to save boaters, swimmers, an occasional drunk sailor and, once, a sheep belonging to August Belmont. For her countless acts of courage, Ida received many honors and tributes including the first gold lifesaving medal from the U.S. government. Her large granite memorial stone, with an emblem of an anchor crossed with oars is inscribed with the words, "The grace darling of America / Keeper of Lime Rock Lighthouse / Newport Harbor / Erected by her many kind friends."

➡ Directions to Common Burying Ground: On the corner of Farewell and Warner streets; the Lewis memorial is just inside the main gate, to the right (easily seen from the street).

Portsmouth, a small town just to the north of Newport, was once the most populous town in the colony. It was settled in 1638 by a band of Puritans banished from Boston—among them, Anne Hutchinson. Along Route 138, the main road connecting the three towns on Aquidneck Island (Newport, Portsmouth and Middletown), is a particularly pretty little church and cemetery.

Portsmouth

St. Mary's Churchyard
Main Street (Route 138)

Harold Stirling Vanderbilt
1884–1970

While most of the famous Vanderbilts who summered in Newport are buried in the family plot in the Moravian Cemetery on Staten Island in New York, at least one, Harold Stirling Vanderbilt, chose to be buried close to the place he loved best. When Harold Vanderbilt died on July 4, 1970, shortly before the start of the America's Cup race, flags on most of the boats in Newport Harbor were lowered to half mast in his honor. He was eulogized at his memorial service a few days later in Newport by the chancellor of Vanderbilt University as "one of the most remarkable men of personal achievement of our century." Among those achievements were his three victories in defending the America's Cup and his title of the "Father of Contract Bridge"—a game that he invented and established a trophy for.

Engraved on his tombstone is a copy of "The Wheel," which he used on all of his yachts and kept as a trophy in his house in Newport.

➡ Directions to St. Mary's Churchyard: Go south on Main Street (Route 138); the grave site is in the southwest section (near the driveway).

Jamestown

Old Friends' Burial Ground
Eldred Road (Route 138)

The little island of Conanicut (9 miles long and 1 to 2 miles across), situated at the mouth of Narragansett Bay, is often called Jamestown, the name of its only town. It was settled in 1656 mostly by Quakers, and many of them are buried in the Old Friends' Burial Ground. Also buried here are many Revolutionary War soldiers who fought valiantly to save their island from the British. One of the most illustrious and best remembered as a war hero is John Eldred, the "one-man army."

John Eldred
1712–1784

Captain John Eldred, a well-to-do retired sea captain, had a farm on Conanicut Island overlooking the East Passage of Narragansett Bay. During the Revolutionary War, snipers on the island tried to protect themselves from the British by firing on enemy boats as they passed

The tombstone of John Eldred, the Yankees' "one man army," at Old Friends' Burial Ground in Jamestown.

the island. Captain Eldred, bolder then most, set up a cannon close to the shore and began doing some serious damage to British vessels. Thinking there was a well-stocked battery here, the British came ashore to take control. To their surprise, they found only the one lone cannon wedged between some rocks (Eldred had quickly escaped to a nearby swamp). They promptly spiked it, thus eliminating Eldred's "one-man army."

➽ **Directions to Old Friends' Burial Ground:** Route 138 cuts across Jamestown from the Newport Bridge to the Jamestown Bridge. The cemetery is located on Route 138 (Eldred Road) about 1 mile before the Jamestown Bridge on the east side of the road. The Eldred grave is toward the back of the cemetery, near the rear stone wall.

Little Compton

Little Compton, nestled in a rural corner of Rhode Island where the Sakonnet River meets the Atlantic Ocean, was one of the earliest settlements in the state. It was originally part of Plymouth Colony and most of the first families were either from Plymouth or Boston. The Commons, where the Old Burying Ground is located and which still occupies most of the center of the village, was laid out in 1675–1677. It contains many interesting old grave sites and monuments, most particularly the one commemorating Elizabeth Pabodie.

The Old Burying Ground on the Commons
Meeting House Lane

Elizabeth Pabodie
1623–1717

Elizabeth Pabodie was the daughter of John and Priscilla Mullins Alden and the first white woman to be born in the New England colonies. The fame of Elizabeth and her parents is due in part to Henry Wadsworth Longfellow's famous poem *The Courtship of Myles Standish.* She led an "exemplary, virtuous and pious life"; had 12 children and, at the time of her death in 1717 at the age of 93 years, she had more than 500 descendants. Many of the families living in and around Little Compton today trace their ancestry back to Elizabeth. The epitaph on her tombstone reads: "A bud from Plymouth's Mayflower sprung / Transplanted here to live and bloom / Her memory ever sweet and young / The centuries guard within."

There are two other burial sites of note here: that of the famous Indian fighter Benjamin Church (1639–1718), who is credited with the death of the infamous King Philip, and two stones in the plot belonging to Simeon Palmer. One of the stones reads, "Here lies Lidia the Wife of Mr. Simeon Palmer, d. 1754 ae. 35" and the other reads, "Here lies Elizabeth who Should have been the Wife of Mr. Simeon Palmer, d. 1776 ae. 64." Epitaph collectors have been trying to figure this one out for more than two centuries!

➺ **Directions to The Old Burying Ground on the Commons:** From Route 138, take Route 77 south into the village of Little Compton. The grave sites are easy to find on the Commons.

CONNECTICUT

This towering memorial marks the grave site of tiny Charles Stratton ("Tom Thumb"),
at Mountain Grove Cemetery in Bridgeport.

Along the Coast

The towns, cities, and villages along Connecticut's 250-mile coastline are defined by their harbors. Large cities such as Stamford, Norwalk, Bridgeport and New Haven began as early coastal ports in the 1630s and 1640s and eventually became some of the state's leading industrial centers. Smaller coastal towns such as Old Lyme, Stonington and Mystic were important shipbuilding and fishing villages and still retain the flavor of their earlier seafaring days. Captains of the sea and captains of industry lie side by side in the many interesting, well-kept cemeteries along Connecticut's shore.

Greenwich

Putnam Cemetery
Parsonage Road

Greenwich, Connecticut, is typical of the attractive, affluent towns that serve as bedroom communities for executives and entertainers who make their living in nearby New York City. It is fitting that a large, beautiful garden cemetery with winding paths and handsome monuments located just off one of the town's quiet country roads is the final resting place for many notable (albeit transplanted) New Englanders. One of the most visited grave sites here is that of a very popular matinee idol of the 1950s, Ezio Pinza.

Ezio Pinza
1895–1957

Nearly 3,000 friends and admirers of Metropolitan Opera singer Ezio Pinza attended his funeral at New York's Cathedral of St. John the Divine. Although the service did not begin until 11:00 A.M., the crowd began to gather in the rain long before the church doors were opened at 7:45. Pinza, after a successful beginning as an opera star in Italy where he was born, came to the Metropolitan Opera Company in 1926; he was hailed as "a majestic figure on the stage, a basso of superb sonority and impressiveness."

In 1949 he shocked his colleagues by leaving the Met to accept a role that many regarded at the time as a gamble and beneath his dignity. It was that of Emil De Becque, the French planter in Rodgers and Hammerstein's *South Pacific*. The musical went on to become one of the all-time Broadway greats, not only winning for Pinza an army of new fans but making him an instant matinee idol.

Movie and television appearances followed, and at the time of his death, after suffering a stroke at the age of 64, some of the most prominent people in the entertainment field acted as honorary pallbearers and participants at his funeral. He was buried in Putnam Cemetery in Greenwich, near Stamford, where he had lived, and his grave is marked with a beautiful, large white headstone.

Among the other noteworthy people buried in Putnam Cemetery are Bud Collyer (1908–1969), a television and radio personality of the 1950s and 1960s (he was the radio voice of Superman); Thomas H. McInnerney (1867–1952), founder of the National Dairy Products Corporation; Colby M. Chester (1877–1965), one of the founders of General Foods Corporation; and architects Theodore Blake (1869–1949) and Thomas Hastings (1860–1929), who designed such monuments as New York Public Library and the House and Senate Buildings in Washington, D.C.

➤➤ **Directions to Putnam Cemetery:** From the center of Greenwich (Route 1), go north on Old Church Road, turn on to Parsonage Road (near Greenwich Country Club). Just inside the gate, take the road to the right (newer section) and the Pinza grave site is on the left.

New Canaan, Redding, Ridgefield

The three small residential towns of New Canaan, Redding and Ridgefield are nestled in between Greenwich and Bridgeport, inland and slightly north of the coast. Many picturesque old cemeteries can be found in this area, and mentioned below is just a sampling of some of the interesting New Englanders buried in the general vicinity.

Lakeview Cemetery
Main Street, New Canaan

A large mausoleum overlooking a duck pond in this small, well-kept garden cemetery denotes the grave site of John Robert Gregg (1864–1948)—educator and inventor of the well-known system of shorthand named for him. Just up the hill from the mausoleum in a shaded corner of the cemetery is a plain headstone simply inscribed with the name Maxwell Everts Perkins (1884–1947). Perkins was a exceptionally talented editor of Charles Scribner's Sons in the early part of the 20th century who took on such young hopefuls as Ernest Hemingway, F. Scott Fitzgerald and Thomas Wolfe. He skillfully polished their first crude writings into best-selling novels.

Another headstone to look for in this cemetery is that of John Rogers (1829–1904), creator of the famous "Rogers group" sculptures. One of his early pieces, *The Slave Auction*, gained great popularity for the abolitionist cause, as did many of his scenes of the Civil War. His later models depicting sentimental scenes of everyday life from 1860 to 1870 were very much in demand at that time and have now become highly valued collector's items.

One other grave site of note in this cemetery is that of Harold T. Webster (1885–1952), the creator of the comic strip "The Timid Soul," featuring Caspar Milquetoast.

➦ **Directions to Lakeview Cemetery:** Take exit 38 off the Merritt Turnpike to the center of New Canaan (Route 123). The cemetery is located at the bottom of Main Street. It is a fairly small cemetery and the grave sites are easy to locate.

Umpawaug Cemetery
Umpawaug Road, Redding

This small cemetery built on the side of a hill along an old country road is not easy to walk through because of its steep slope. But at its summit, on flat ground, is a pair of headstones marking the graves of two men whose names, although not exactly household words, have nevertheless made significant contributions to the American way of life. One marks the grave of Albert Bigelow Paine (1861–1937) and the other, that of Beardsley Ruml (1894–1960). Paine, friend and editor of Mark Twain, was the author of a three-volume biography of Mark Twain and editor of Twain's letters. But he is best remembered for his novel *The Great White Way* (1901), which was responsible for giving Broadway its world-famous nickname. Beardsley Ruml, on the other hand, was a social scientist, educator, businessman and tax planner who devised a method in 1943 for the pay-as-you-go plan for federal income tax. We have him to thank for inventing the withholding tax!

➻ **Directions to Umpawaug Cemetery:** From Route 53 (Bethel-Redding Road) in Redding, take a left onto Umpawaug Road at the fire station. The cemetery is about 1 mile down this road on the right.

St. Mary's Cemetery
Copps Hill Road, Ridgefield

Cyril Ritchard (1898–1977) was an actor to the end. He suffered a heart attack on stage during a matinee performance of *Side by Side by Sondheim* in 1978 and died soon after. Australian born, he began performing on the stage when he was in his teens, and his distinctive voice and comedic style were a natural for musical comedy. He stared in many Broadway and London musicals (some with his wife, Midge Elliot; together they were dubbed "the musical Lunts"), but Ritchard will always be remembered as the wicked Captain Hook in the classic Broadway musical *Peter Pan*. Archbishop Fulton J. Sheen of New York presided at the Catholic mass in honor of Ritchard at St. Mary's Roman Catholic Church in Ridgefield, and he was buried beside his wife in the church cemetery.

➻ **Directions to St. Mary's Cemetery:** Copps Hill Road is off Main Street in the center of Ridgefield. Go to the end of the street and you will find the cemetery on the corner.

Bridgeport   *Mountain Grove Cemetery*
2675 North Avenue

Bridgeport has long been regarded as the chief industrial city of the state producing, over the years, everything from whalebone corsets to helicopters. It has always attracted the leading captains of industry and entrepreneurs to its shores, and many of them who have left their mark on the city are buried in Mountain Grove Cemetery.

One of the most impressive and well-visited grave sites in this large cemetery is that of the most colorful entrepreneur of them all, Phineas T. Barnum, producer of "The Greatest Show on Earth." Buried just across the road from Barnum is his most famous performer, Charles S. Stratton—better known as "Tom Thumb."

Phineas T. Barnum
1810–1891

Born in the small town of Bethel, Connecticut, on July 5, 1810, P. T. Barnum was to become known the world over as the greatest showman of his day. In 1842 he opened a large museum in New York City featuring such living oddities as a "Mermaid from Feejee," a "Twenty-Five-Inch Man" (Tom Thumb), "The Bearded Lady" and "The Siamese Twins" (Chang and Eng). The museum became an instant success and was visited by thousands of people, including such notables as Charles Dickens, Henry James and Edward, prince of Wales.

In his sixties, Barnum opened "The Greatest Show on Earth," the first great American traveling circus. He later combined his talents with those of James Anthony Bailey to produce "The Barnum and Bailey Circus." When it played in London, Queen Victoria herself attended.

Gravely ill in the spring of 1891 with what was diagnosed as acute congestion of the brain, and knowing he was about to die, he made arrangements for a modest funeral. His love of publicity, however, made him so curious about his obituary that the *Evening Sun* of New York was given permission to publish his obituary in advance so that he might enjoy it. On March

The graveside monument of Phineas Barnum, co-owner of Barnum and Bailey's famous traveling circus, is in Mountain Grove Cemetery, Bridgeport.

14, the headline read: "Great and Only Barnum. He Wanted To Read His Obituary; Here It Is."

Three weeks later Barnum died at his home in Bridgeport, Connecticut, telling his wife, Nancy, "My last thoughts are of you." On April 7, thousands of people crowded about the South Congregational Church to hear him tearfully eulogized. From the church, the funeral cortege wended slowly along the mile distance, past flags at half mast, to Mountain Grove Cemetery, where he was laid to rest beside his first wife, Charity. A large granite monument with stairs leading up to it marks his grave site. A large statue of him, presented to Bridgeport by Bailey and members of the circus, stands in Seaside Park.

Charles S. Stratton
"General Tom Thumb"
1838–1886

The five-year-old Charles Stratton was discovered by P. T. Barnum on an early trip to Bridgeport, Connecticut, in 1842. The boy was a perfectly formed midget and only 25 inches tall. Although normal in all ways at birth, he had stopped growing after his first birthday. At that time, medical science knew little to nothing about the function of the pituitary gland, which controls the growth hormones.

The Stratton family was poor and the great showman easily convinced the family to let Charles join Barnum at his museum in New York. Under Barnum's tutelage and dressed in appropriate garb, Charles impersonated such popular figures as Napoleon, Goliath and Cupid and became an instant success. He later traveled to Europe with Barnum, where Charles, as General Tom Thumb, was royally received, giving several command performances before Queen Victoria in London. He was also entertained by the king and queen in Paris, and attended bullfights in Spain with Queen Isabella.

At the age of 23, Stratton married 32-inch-tall Lavinia Warren. Approximately 2,000 people attended the wedding, and afterward, the couple was received by President and Mrs. Lincoln at the White House. They were happily married for 20 years. The general eventually grew portly and attained the height of 3 feet 4 inches.

Charles Stratton died of apoplexy at the age of 45 on July 15, 1883, and more than 10,000 people attended his funeral service. He was laid to rest in Mountain Grove Cemetery, across the way from Barnum's grave site. (See photograph, page 81.) He had commissioned his own memorial, a 40-foot marble shaft with a life-size granite statue of himself on the top. Next to his memorial, a small headstone with the words "His Wife," marks the small grave of Lavinia who died in 1919, at the age of 78.

➤➤ **Directions to Mountain Grove Cemetery:** Follow Route 1 (North Avenue) west of the town center to

Dewey Street. The grave sites of Barnum and Stratton are along the main path to the right as you enter and are quite visible.

St. John's Cemetery   **Stratford**
Nichols Avenue

Igor Ivanovich Sikorsky
1889–1972

As the town of Kittyhawk, North Carolina, is forever linked with the name of the Wright brothers, so is the town of Stratford, Connecticut, linked with the name Igor Ivanovitch Sikorsky. This legendary aviation pioneer is buried only a few miles from the landing strip where he piloted the world's first practical helicopter, a spindly aircraft he himself had designed. He founded the Sikorsky Aero Engineering Corporation in Stratford in the early 1920s, building Pan American Airline's flying boat—the plane that began the era of transoceanic passenger service. But it is the development of the helicopter and his vision of its potential as a viable military, commercial and civilian flying craft that he is most noted for.

Sikorsky died of a heart attack on October 26, 1972, at the age of 83. On the day of his funeral in Stratford, representatives of the U.S. Army, Navy, Coast Guard and Marines flew four different models of Sikorsky helicopters over St. John's Cemetery during the funeral services.

➦ **Directions to St. John's Cemetery:** From the Merritt Parkway, take the Nichols Avenue exit (Route 108), and the cemetery is on the left just before the Trumbull town line.

Mount Carmel   **Hamden**
Whitney Avenue

The industrial development of Hamden dates back to 1798 when the famous inventor Eli Whitney set up shop here. He and many other such illustrious individuals are buried in the larger, nearby city of New Haven. But here in Hamden, far from the center of town in a small, quiet cemetery is buried one of the country's foremost playwrights, Thornton Wilder.

Thornton Wilder
1897–1975

Mount Carmel is a small country cemetery, the kind of place Thornton Wilder, playwright and novelist, might have had in mind when he wrote his famous play *Our Town.* On a cold December day, a group of mourners—family members and close friends—gathered in the rain on a hilly slope to pay their last respects to Wilder, who had died of a heart attack in his sleep two days before. Thornton's brother, the Reverend Dr. Amos N. Wilder, of Harvard Divinity School, and the Reverend William Sloan Coffin, Jr., chaplain of Yale University, conducted the service.

A few weeks later, a large memorial service was held at the Battel Chapel at Yale University with much praise for this three-time winner of the Pulitzer Prize and the first recipient of the National Medal for Literature. Wilder's novels and plays dealt with what he construed as the universal verities in human nature such as pride, avarice and envy. "I am not interested in the ephemeral—such as the adulteries of dentists," he once said. "I am interested in those things that repeat, and repeat, and repeat in the lives of the millions." A tall, handsome stone (designed by Thornton's mother) marks the family burial plot in this old cemetery.

➤ **Directions to Mount Carmel:** The cemetery is approximately 8 miles north from the town green in Hamden on Whitney Avenue. The grave site is at the far end of the cemetery on the slope of the hill.

West Haven　　*Oak Grove Cemetery*
Spring Street

Just before crossing the West River into the city of New Haven you find the small residential suburb of West

Haven. It was settled in 1638, so it follows that its cemeteries date back to its early history. Buried in the oldest cemetery in town, Oak Grove, is one of New England's quintessential Yankees, Rufus Porter.

Rufus Porter
1792–1884

Born in Boxford, Massachusetts, Rufus Porter spent much of his life traveling throughout New England. He worked as a painter, schoolmaster, cobbler, fiddler, coast guardsman and at other odd jobs. These occupations, however, only sustained him while Porter pursued his real talent, that of inventing. Some of his inventions showed great promise, such as a design for a passenger-carrying flight machine (long before the Wright brothers were born), a washing machine, a fire alarm system, a life preserver and a revolving rifle (he sold the plans for the latter to Samuel Colt).

Although he never stayed in one place long enough for any of his ideas to be carried through, Porter is still very well known and admired throughout New England as an itinerant painter. He not only painted portraits of many New Englanders but left his now-famous murals on more than 100 houses in several New England states. These houses, many of them owned by local historical societies and open to the public, are highly prized for their original Rufus Porter murals.

➼ **Directions to Oak Grove Cemetery:** From I-95 take exit 43 west. The cemetery is directly on the left; enter on Spring Street (the first left turn).

New Haven

Grove Street Cemetery
Grove Street

New Haven was one of the first planned communities in America, being laid out by the Puritans in nine equal squares. The central square, the town green, is still one of the liveliest spots in town as it is surrounded by the campus of Yale University. In the late 18th and early 19th centuries New Haven was a thriving port and manufacturing town. Many industrialists, inventors and educators made their homes here, and some of the most illustrious were buried in Grove Street Cemetery. This large, formal cemetery, laid out in 1797, is entered through a massive brownstone gate. Just inside the gate is a map showing the location of the numerous grave sites of notables buried here. (A copy of this map is also available in the cemetery office.)

Noah Webster
1758–1843

Noah Webster, the "Schoolmaster to America," was born on a small farm in West Hartford, Connecticut. (His house, restored and preserved, is now a National Historic Landmark and open to the public.) His first publication, the *American Spelling Book,* called the "Blue-backed Speller," became the standard guide to spelling and composition for generations of American schoolchildren. But it was his masterpiece *An American Dictionary of the English Language,* which he created alone and by hand, that made the name *Webster* forever synonymous with the word *dictionary.* Through its numerous editions it has outsold every book in the English language except the Bible.

Webster was 67 years old when he completed the dictionary, but he continued to write and publish until the year he died (of pneumonia) at the age of 85. His last words as he lay on his deathbed were, "I have struggled with many difficulties. Some I have been able to overcome, and by some I have been overcome. I have made many mistakes, but I love my country, and I trust no precept of mine has taught any dear youth to sin."

Two well-attended memorial services were held in his honor, one at the Center Church in New Haven and the other at Amherst College (which he helped to found) in Massachusetts.

Eli Whitney
1765–1925

Most schoolchildren know that Eli Whitney invented the cotton gin—the machine that drastically changed the way of life in the South. But it was also an invention that he spent most of his life defending through the courts when others copied his idea. His invention brought great wealth to many others, but little to Whitney himself who went heavily into debt defending his patent in the courts. To recoup his loses he began making muskets for the government. He saw the need to substitute duplicate, interchangeable parts for handmade parts, thus laying the foundation for mass-production methods that would eventually industrialize society.

He died a wealthy man and was buried with great honor. Because he was one of the most eminent citizens of New Haven and the founder of its largest industry, it isn't surprising that such places as Whitney Avenue, Whitneyville and Lake Whitney were named for him. His large tomb in the Grove Street Cemetery is inscribed, "Eli Whitney. The Inventor of the Cotton Gin. Of useful Science and Arts, the efficient Patron and Improver. In the social relations of life, a Model of excellence."

Charles Goodyear
1800–1860

The name *Goodyear* is practically synonymous with *rubber*, yet Charles Goodyear, who invented the vulcanization process for rubber that made it a highly profitable commercial product, died heavily in debt. He actually spent several years in debtor's prison, where he carried out many of his experiments.

In the mid-1820s, when his father's hardware business in New Haven went bankrupt, Goodyear began experimenting with rubber. At that time rubber products were far from perfect; in summer they melted and in the winter they hardened and cracked. He accidentally discovered the vulcanization process when, during one of his experiments, he dropped a blob of a rubber/sulfur mixture on a hot stove. When the blob cooled, he found that it was a hard, firm, yet pliable substance. Goodyear quickly patented the product, but his idea was soon pirated. He filed suit and was defended in court by the famous Daniel Webster. He won the patent suit, but Webster's fee of $25,000 was more than Goodyear himself was ever to gain from his own efforts.

In May 1860, broken in health and finance, Goodyear was on his way to New Haven from Washington, D.C., to visit his seriously ill daughter when he himself became gravely ill. He died in a hotel in New York the day after his daughter's death. His body was brought to New Haven for burial. His estate was $200,000 in arrears at the time of his death.

Other noteworthy grave sites in Grove Street Cemetery are those of prominent former presidents, professors, scholars and sports figures of Yale University such as Jedediah Morse (1761–1826), "Father of American Geography"; Josiah Willard Gibbs, Jr. (1839–1903), "Father of Thermodynamics"; Lyman Beecher (1775–1863), clergyman, abolitionist and father of Harriet Beecher Stowe; and Walter Camp (1859–1925), Yale's famous football coach who has also been called the "Father of American Football."

➡ **Directions to Grove Street Cemetery:** Grove Street Cemetery (also known as the New Haven Burying Ground) is in the heart of downtown New Haven on Grove Street. A map to the grave sites is available at the cemetery office.

Evergreen Cemetery
Evergreen Avenue

In nearby Evergreen Cemetery are the graves of Bob Kiphuth (1890–1967), Yale's outstanding swimming coach whose team won 528 meets (losing only 12) during his career, and those of the Winchester family whose fortune was made in the manufacturing of firing arms. Oliver Winchester (1810–1880) created the repeating rifle and the side-loading Winchester rifle. His daughter-in-law, Sarah Pardee (1837–1922), became an eccentric in her later years and felt she had to atone for those who were killed by Winchester rifles. Guided by spirits, she began building a house (now called the "Mystery House" and open to the public in San Jose, California). The "spirits" told her that as long as she continued to build the house she would not die. By the time she did die, of natural causes at the age of 85, the house contained more than 160 rooms. She was buried in the family plot in New Haven.

➤➤ **Directions to Evergreen Cemetery:** Evergreen Cemetery is at the intersection of Route 1 (Evergreen Avenue) and Ella Grasso Boulevard. A maps to the grave sites is available at the cemetery office.

Evergreen Cemetery **Killingworth**
Green Hill Road

Hugh Lofting
1886–1947

This small cemetery on a backcountry road in Connecticut is in sight of the home where Hugh Lofting lived and wrote his famous children's stories about a kindly animal doctor known as "Dr. Dolittle" that have charmed both children and adults for many decades. The stories, at least one of which won the distinguished Newbery Medal, grew from a series of illustrated letters Lofting had written to his children when he was at the front during World War I. At the time of his death his wife, Josephine (now buried next to him), received letters of condolence from children all over the world who spoke poignantly of their sense of loss at his death. Lofting's friend Sir Hugh Walpole predicted that Dr. Dolittle would go down through the centuries "as a kind of Pied Piper with thousands of children at his heels."

His small, plain headstone is inscribed with his name and dates and the Latin phrase *Quis Separabit* (Who Shall Separate Us).

➤➤ **Directions to Evergreen Cemetery:** The cemetery is located in the Southwest District of Killingworth just over the boundary of the town of Madison (Route 81).

Ye Townes Antientist Burial Ground **New London**
Huntington Street

The city of New London, situated near the mouth of the Thames River on Long Island Sound, has a long maritime history. It was laid out in 1646 by John Winthrop, and early settlers were attracted to its busy deep-water port of entry.

During the Revolution it became an important scene of military action, and in spite of being set afire by Benedict Arnold and his troops in 1781, many pre-Revolutionary buildings still exist today. Among the old relics remaining is Ye Townes Antientist Burial Ground, where many soldiers and sailors of early wars are buried. Here also is the grave of one Sarah Kemble Knight, whose famous *Private Journal of a Journey from Boston to New York in the Year 1704* is a valuable slice of early American history.

Sarah Kemble Knight
1666–1727

No one knows for sure just why Sarah Kemble Knight, a widowed Boston schoolteacher, set off one October day in 1702 and traveled round trip from Boston to New York on horseback. The 271-mile journey through wild and unsettled countryside, taking her five months to complete, was one that few stalwart men would even attempt to do in those days. But through all kinds of weather, misadventures, sickness and lack of sleep, Sarah pressed on toward her destination, recording her adventures in a diary.

Sarah's diary recounts in witty detail the different habits and customs of the regions she visited and the total lack of proper accommodations for travelers along the way. In 1714 she moved to New London and set up her own inn, presumably one with good food and clean sheets. Her diary was discovered and published in 1825, almost 100 years after her death, and has continued to be an entertaining source of information about the early customs of 18th-century southern New England.

➥ **Directions to Ye Townes Antientist Burial Ground:** From I-95, take exit 83 east onto Huntington Street. The cemetery is small and the Knight marker is easy to find.

Uncas
"Last of the Mohicans"
c.1606–c.1683

Contrary to the theme of James Fenimore Cooper's classic novel *The Last of the Mohicans,* a band of about 600 of these native Americans (actually their relations, the Mohegans) still gather for an annual homecoming in Uncasville, Connecticut, every August. The town is named for Uncas, the grand sachem of the Mohegans, a powerful tribe that once occupied all of southern Connecticut. (Cooper used Uncas as the model for his novel.) Not much of the old proud tribe remains here, but there is a small museum, a church and the ancient burial ground with the monument and grave of Chief Uncas. Fort Shantok State Park where the burial ground is located is the site of the last siege against the Mohegans by the Narragansett Indians in 1645. Aided by the British, Uncas was able to withstand the attack, thus the Mohegans emerged as the only important tribe in southern New England.

➡ **Directions to Fort Shantok Indian Burying Ground:** From I-95 take Route 32 to Uncasville and then to Fort Shantok State Park (well marked). The cemetery, enclosed by a split-rail fence, is visible from the parking lot.

Evergreen Cemetery   **Stonington**
North Main Street

Stephen Vincent Benét
1898–1943

The small, picturesque seafaring village of Stonington, close to the Connecticut border, has long attracted artists and writers. One of the most celebrated to be buried here is the American poet and author Stephen Vincent

Benét. He published his first volumes of verse when he was 17 and his Pultzer Prize–winning poem *John Brown's Body* when he was 29. This was followed by a number of works, including his classic short story "The Devil and Daniel Webster." Benét died suddenly of a heart attack in New York City at the age of 44 years. At the time of his death, he was in the midst of writing a series of five books of verse on the American West, but had only completed one. In 1944 he was awarded the Pulitzer Prize posthumously for this work, *Western Star.*

➤➤ **Directions to Evergreen Cemetery:** Evergreen Cemetery is located on the south corner of Route 1 and North Main Street. The grave site is located on the east side of the cemetery.

Greater Hartford Area

The term *Yankee* as it applies to many New Englanders actually began in the Hartford area of Connecticut. When the English Puritans from Massachusetts moved in on the Dutch fur trappers who had already settled here in the late 1630s, the Dutch used the term *Jankees* (a combination of *Jan* and *cheese* meaning "John Cheese") in a derogative way to describe them. No one knows for sure just what the name implied, but New Englanders now take pride in the term, which has come to describe a combination of such admirable character traits as honesty, thriftiness, frugality, straightforwardness and, perhaps most important, ingenuity. You'll find the grave sites of many such Yankees in the Hartford area.

Hartford   *Center Church Graveyard*
Main and Gold Streets

Hartford, the capital city of Connecticut, was the site of one of the earliest and strongest colonial centers. Although Dutch traders had originally built a trading post here in 1633, it was actually settled as an English colony in 1636 when Thomas Hooker brought his congregation here from Massachusetts. They built their first meetinghouse on what is now the corner of Main and Gold streets and Hooker was pastor there until his death in 1647. Today, standing on the same spot, is the fourth structure, the First Church of Christ, built in 1807 which closely resembles the Christopher Wren church St. Martin's-in-the-Fields in London. The adjacent ancient burying ground, begun in 1640, is the site of the graves of the city's early leaders including Hooker.

Thomas Hooker
1586–1647

Thomas Hooker was a clergyman who ran into trouble first in England and than in Massachusetts for his nonconformist views. He objected to the rule that church membership was required in order to vote. He finally fled to Hartford where he and his followers found the religious freedom and democracy they had been seeking. In 1639 the Fundamental Orders of Connecticut, largely framed by Hooker, were formally adopted as the basic law of the Connecticut Colony. It was the first written state constitution known in U.S. history, giving Connecticut's its now-popular nickname, "The Constitution State."

The ancient burying ground behind Center Church still retains many of the original gravestones of the early settlers, some dating all the way back to the 17th century. It is believed that Thomas Hooker was buried either under or near the northwest corner of the present church. A large plaque over the probable grave site pays homage to Hooker: "A leader of the founders of his commonwealth / A preacher of persuasive power / A statesman who based all civil authority on the free consent of the people."

➼ **Directions to Center Church Graveyard:** The cemetery is in the center of downtown Hartford on Main Street. It is reached from I-84 or I-91 by taking the downtown Hartford exit.

Cedar Hill Cemetery
453 Fairfield Avenue

Cedar Hill Cemetery, founded in 1864, was one of the first "rural" cemeteries in the country. This was a new concept in the mid-19th century, catering to the patriarchal Victorian family. Rather than the rectilinear grid pattern of the pre–Civil War burying grounds, the rural cemetery took on a landscaped parklike setting with family plots centered around an obelisk or statue. Elaborate monuments to the deceased became very popular at that time, and as Hartford was the headquarters for one of the leading monument firms, the New England Granite Works, Cedar Hill is filled with many elegant memorials. Many prominent Hartford families are represented here, including such well-known names as Samuel Colt (1814–1862), firearms manufacturer who invented the revolver that helped win the West; J. P. Morgan (1837–1913), powerful American financier and industrialist at the turn of the 20th century; Isabella Beecher Hooker (1822–1907), a prominent figure in the women's rights movement of her day; Thomas Gallaudet (1787–1851), the founding teacher at the American School for the Deaf, the first institution in the Western Hemisphere for the benefit of the handicapped; and Gilbert F. Heublein (1849–1937), who developed bottled cocktails and brought A.1. sauce and Smirnoff vodka to the United States.

Samuel Colt
1814–1862

When Samuel Colt died, his obituary in *The Hartford Times* read, "In the death of Col. Colt, Hartford loses her most enterprising and public spirited citizen. To his liberal and sagacious enterprises, more than to the work of any other one man, or set of men, is the prosperity of this city due."

Not only had Colt built his very successful arms factory (manufacturing the Colt revolver, which is credited as "the gun that won the West") in Hartford but he surrounded it with housing and recreational facilities for his employees and their families. His early death of "an attack upon the brain," at the age of 47 came as a shock to the city.

His funeral was described by one reporter as the most spectacular ever seen in Hartford: "It was like the last act of a grand opera, with threnodial music played by Colt's own band of immigrant German craftsmen, supported by a silent chorus of bereaved townsfolk. Crepe bands on their left arms, Colt's 1,500 workmen filed in pairs past the metallic casket in the parlor of Armsmear, his ducal mansion. . . ." Following a simple Episcopal service, the workers formed two parallel lines and various groups of Connecticut militia, "drums muffled, colors draped, and arms reversed," marched between them to a small, private graveyard on the property as thousands of mourners looked on. (His body was later moved to the present site at Cedar Hill.)

John Pierpont Morgan
1837–1913

News about the death of J. P. Morgan, considered the most powerful figure in American finance and industry (he once lent $65 million in gold to a financially strapped U.S. government) ran for days on the front page of newspapers across the country. Wall Street was draped with flags hung at half mast from nearly every building and the Stock Exchange was closed during his funeral services. Actually there were three services: one in the Grand Hotel in Rome, Italy, where he died while on vacation; one in New York City and the third in Hartford (where he was born). Even in Rome, the flags were flown at half mast and throngs of people lined the streets near the hotel and stood silently as the hearse bearing his body left for the harbor where a ship awaited to take him home.

Months before he died, Morgan had written down the arrangements he wished for his funeral—a simple service with no eulogy. Invitations to the service at St. George's Episcopal Church in New York City were much sought after and the church was filled to its capacity of 1,500. Representatives from many major institutions in the country were in attendance and floral tributes from world leaders, including the king of Italy and the German emperor, were banked around the chancel. A phalanx of police and mounted guards were needed to control the large crowds of people who had come to glimpse the distinguished guests.

The body was brought to Hartford by a special railroad car, and once again, crowds had gathered and flags throughout the city were flown at half mast. Burial took place in the family plot at Cedar Hill Cemetery. The plot is at the summit of a hill with cedar and maple trees scattered about. In its center is an 8-foot-high obelisk of polished red granite. Inscribed on it, along with the names of several generations of Morgans are the words, "For if we have been planted together in the likeness of His death, we shall be also in the likeness of His resurrection."

➤ **Directions to Cedar Hill Cemetery:** The cemetery is located on the south side of Hartford at the intersection of Maple and Fairfield avenues (Berlin Turnpike, Route 5). A map and guide to the burial grounds are available at the cemetery office just inside the gate.

Old North Cemetery
1821 Main Street

Frederick Law Olmsted
1822–1903

Another grave site of note in Hartford is that of Frederick Law Olmsted. He was born in Hartford but lived most of his life in Brookline, Massachusetts (where his home has been preserved and is now open to the public). A world-renowned landscape architect, he is best remembered for his work on New York's Central Park and as the designer of park systems in other major cities, particularly Boston. He died quietly at McLean Hospital in Waverly, Massachusetts, at the age of 81 years with his devoted son, Frederick Law Olmsted, Jr., at his bedside. A private funeral service was held and without ceremony or mourners, his ashes were deposited in the family vault in the Old North Cemetery.

➤ **Directions to Old North Cemetery:** The cemetery is located on the north side of Hartford about a 5-minute drive from downtown (following Main Street to the north).

Fairview Cemetery　**West Hartford**
Pleasant Street

Frederick Rentschler
(1887–1956)

Known as "Mr. Horsepower," Frederick Rentschler, founder of Pratt and Whitney, is credited as the man whose engines furnished one-half of America's airborne piston horsepower during World War II. He devoted his life to making bigger, better, more powerful airplane engines to help give the United States an air force second to none. He was often quoted as saying, "There is no such thing as a second-best air force. There is the best—or nothing."

➤ **Directions to Fairview Cemetery:** From Route 84 to South Main Street, turn west onto Farmington Avenue. Pleasant Street is about six streets up on the east side of Farmington Avenue. The cemetery is at the end of the street.

Riverside Cemetery　**Farmington**
Maple Street

Farmington is one of the most attractive suburbs of Hartford. Settled in 1640, most of the center of this picturesque town is now an historic district. Beautiful, old, large, white clapboard houses line Main Street—some of them now dormitories for the internationally famous Miss Porter's School. Among the many distinguished families that have lived here is that of William Gillette, the actor famous for his portrayal of Sherlock Holmes.

William Gillette
"Sherlock Holmes"
1853–1937

William Gillette, actor and playwright, was credited with popularizing realism in dramatic writing and staging. But he is best remembered for his famous stage performances as "the hawk-faced man of action," Detective Sherlock Holmes. He is also well known to the thousands of visitors who frequent the medieval castle he built for himself in 1919 in Hadlyme, on the Connecticut River, and left as a memorial to the state. When he died in 1937, many tributes praising his skills as an actor and playwright were published in the *New York Times* from the leading drama societies. He was lauded as "a great actor and a great gentleman of the old school." He died from complications after suffering a cold and was buried in Farmington (where he was born) with a simple private service.

➤➤ **Directions to Riverside Cemetery:** Riverside Cemetery is at the end of Maple Street, one block west of Main Street (Route 10), just south of the village center. The grave site is well marked.

Wethersfield   *Emanuel Synagogue Cemetery*
Berlin Turnpike

Sophie Tucker
1884–1966

Called "The Last of the Red Hot Mamas," Sophie Tucker was a large, buxom blond, bedecked in flashy gold-sequined dresses, who could belt out torch songs with great gusto. She began singing for nickels and dimes when she was very young in her family's diner in Hartford. She went on to become a popular star in vaudeville and burlesque, and when vaudeville collapsed, she brought her act to night clubs. She appeared frequently on television in her sixties and seventies and was immediately recognized by her signature song, "Some of These Days."

When Tucker died of lung cancer in 1966 more than 1,000 people crowded Riverside Chapel in New York City to hear her eulogized by George Jessel, another popular vaudeville entertainer and Broadway star. She was "loved and respected from the tipsters to the tycoons," Jessel said, "from a chambermaid in a small hotel to the queen of England in Buckingham Palace." (In honor of the singer, striking funeral car drivers removed their picket lines from in front of the chapel during the hour-long service.) Her body was taken by a special car to Hartford where another service, attended by 500 people, was held before her burial in Emanuel Cemetery.

➤➤ **Directions to Emanuel Synagogue Cemetery:** Emanuel Synagogue Cemetery is located on the Berlin Turnpike (Route 5) in Wethersfield.

Nathan Hale Cemetery Coventry
Routes 31 and 275

The northeast section of Connecticut, not far from the capital city of Hartford, is called Connecticut's "Quiet Corner." Yet, in the midst of this peaceful, rolling countryside were born some of the state's most illustrious and fiery heroes whose historical actions and deeds in the late 18th century echoed loudly across the nation. One such person was Nathan Hale, the official hero of Connecticut, born and raised in the sleepy little town of Coventry. Although he was buried in an unknown grave somewhere in Manhattan where he was hung in 1776, his special memorial is located in the family cemetery in his home town of Coventry.

Nathan Hale
1755–1776

Dominating the center of Coventry village is the large stone memorial dedicated to the patriot Nathan Hale, Connecticut's most famous son. The monument, erected in 1846 for the 70th anniversary of Captain Hale's death, is made of 25 tons of stone and is 14 feet square at the base and 45 feet high. Hale was born in Coventry and became a schoolteacher, but he joined the Connecticut Militia at the outbreak of the Revolutionary War. In 1776, at the age of 21, Hale volunteered to undertake a dangerous espionage trip to New York. He was captured by the British and executed without a trial and his body was buried at an unknown place in Manhattan. Just before he was hung, his now-famous last words were uttered: "I only regret that I have but one life to lose for my country." These words are inscribed on the monument. Members of Hale's family are all buried in the family lot (behind the cenotaph to the right), where another special dedication stone to honor Nathan and his brother was erected by their father.

➽ **Directions to Nathan Hale Cemetery:** The cemetery is located in the center of the village of Coventry, at the intersection of Routes 31 and 275.

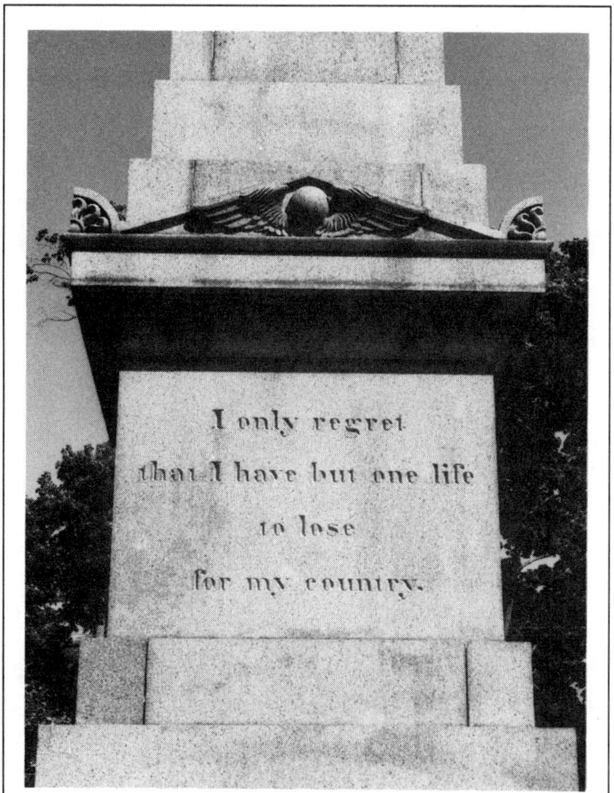

Nathan Hale's massive stone memorial towers over the center of Coventry.

Another small, peaceful town in Connecticut's Quiet Corner, Lebanon belies its militant activities of Revolutionary War days. At that time its location was on one of the main routes between Boston and New York, and it became a supply lifeline for Revolutionary War troops. The Trumbull family store, still standing in the center of town, was transformed into the Revolutionary War Office where hundreds of secret meetings and activities of the Committee of Safety were held.

Jonathan Trumbull
1769–1785

Three governors of Connecticut, all of them members of the prosperous Trumbull family, are buried in the Trumbull cemetery. The most famous one, "Brother Jonathan," as he was called by George Washington, was the only colonial governor to side openly with the patriots. During the Revolutionary War, as a close friend and advisor to General Washington, Trumbull was one of the chief organizers of food, clothing and munitions supplies for Washington's army.

His home (open to the public) still stands in the center of town. The second-floor bedroom where he took refuge when a price was set on his head, has no windows except for a small, shuttered opening high above the governor's desk. Just to the left of this opening is the "sentry box" where a man stood on guard day and night to protect the governor. Trumbull was governor of Connecticut from 1769 until just 15 months before his death in 1785 at the age of 75.

Also buried in Trumbull Cemetery is William Williams, a signer of the Declaration of Independence and husband of Trumbull's daughter, Mary. (Trumbull's son, John, known as "the painter of the Revolution" and of the murals in the Capitol rotunda, is buried in New Haven beneath the art gallery that he designed at Yale University.)

➤➤ **Directions to Trumbull Cemetery:** The cemetery is located about ³/₄ mile east of the village of Lebanon on Route 207 at the corner of Kick Hill Road.

Western Connecticut

The scenic hills and valleys of this part of Connecticut are dotted with small traditional New England villages. Many of these towns, particularly in the northwestern region, were once highly industrialized due to the rich deposits of iron ore in the area. As the industries moved away, nature quickly reclaimed the land, and it is now considered one of the most unspoiled and picturesque areas of the state. Many well-known people were born and bred in this lovely spot—some moved away—but many came home to be buried.

Cornwall

Cornwall Hollow Cemetery
Route 43

Mark Van Doren
1894–1972
Carl Van Doren
1885–1950

Mark Van Doren was considered a "teacher's teacher." On the day of his funeral in the little village of Cornwall where more than 600 people gathered to pay homage to this Pulitzer Prize–winning poet, critic and teacher, the Cornwall Public School was closed for the day. Although native to Illinois, Cornwall had been home to three generations of the Van Doren family, and Carl lived here for much of his life.

Mark's poetry was about man and nature, and during his lifetime he was frequently compared with Robert Frost. He was highly thought of at Columbia University where he was a professor for many years. Among Mark's devoted students were such diverse and aspiring writers as Thomas Merton, Allen Ginsberg, John Berryman, Clifton Fadiman, Lionel Trilling and Jack Kerouac.

("Kerouac," according to Ginsberg, "quit the Columbia football team to spend more time studying Shakespeare with Van Doren.")

Mark's brother, Carl, was also a Columbia professor and a Pulitzer Prize winner (for his biography of Benjamin Franklin) and was founder and editor of the *Literary Guild*. When Carl died in 1950 his ashes were scattered at Wickshire, his home, which is just a short distance away from the small country cemetery where Mark is buried.

➠ **Directions to Cornwall Hollow Cemetery:** From Route 7 in West Cornwall, take 128 east to Route 43. Cornwall Hollow Cemetery is across the street from a small church.

Hillside Cemetery **Thomaston**
Main Street

Seth Thomas
1785–1859

Seth Thomas and Eli Terry were clockmakers in Plymouth Hollow, Connecticut. They worked together for a while, but eventually each set up his own factory in different parts of town. After they died, one part of Plymouth became Thomaston and another part became Terryville, renamed in their honor.

In the early 1800s, clocks were made entirely by hand and were thus a luxury. Few homes had clocks until Thomas perfected methods of mass production in his factory. His company, still in operation today, brought clocks within the price range of most families and became known throughout the world.

There are many descendants of Seth Thomas living today (at least three with the same name) and many branches of the family buried in this old cemetery.

➠ **Directions to Hillside Cemetery:** Go south on Main Street to Route 254, turning right at the traffic light; the next left turn will take you into the cemetery. The Seth Thomas grave is in the southwest corner near the woods.

Roxbury

Roxbury Center Cemetery
Route 67

Manfred Lee
1905–1971

Manfred Lee collaborated with his cousin Frederic Dannay to create one of the most famous detectives of all time, "Ellery Queen." Together the two men wrote 33 Ellery Queen novels and an Ellery Queen magazine and provided the format for many radio and television shows. Under the pseudonym of "Barnaby Ross," they also collaborated on a second series of detective stories called Drury Lane. They were considered among the top mystery writers of their day and maintained an exceptionally high standard of writing throughout their careers. Both writers hated violence of any kind, and their heroes were noted for solving crimes by their "brilliant deductions."

Lee, who lived on a 63-acre estate in Roxbury, had declared his property a game preserve—with no hunting allowed. He died en route to the hospital after suffering a heart attack at his home. A private funeral service was held in Roxbury, and he is buried in the Roxbury Center Cemetery.

➻ **Directions to Roxbury Center Cemetery:** The cemetery is located in Roxbury Center on Route 67.

Woodbury

New North Cemetery
Route 317

Leroy Anderson
1908–1975

In the 1930s, while working on a doctoral thesis on foreign languages and fully intending to become a teacher, Leroy Anderson began conducting and arranging music for the Harvard Band. This soon led to his giving up his thesis and becoming a free-lance conductor, composer and arranger in the Boston and New York area.

The gravestone of Leroy Anderson, innovative conductor, composer and arranger, at New North Cemetery in Woodbury.

His unusual style of combining popular music with symphonic elements caught the attention of Arthur Fiedler, renowned conductor of the Boston Pops Orchestra. Fiedler quickly hired the young innovator, and Anderson's popular compositions for the Pops such as "Jazz Pizzicato," "Fiddle-Faddle" and "The Syncopated Clock" launched him on his way to becoming America's best known semiclassical composer. In 1952, his composition "Blue Tango" made him an instant celebrity when it became the first strictly instrumental number to reach the top of the Hit Parade.

He was once quoted as saying, "I never aimed for success or money or fame. I just did what I wanted to do. It turned out that people liked it." A large, square granite stone with a small American flag by its side marks his grave in this well-kept cemetery.

➤ **Directions to New North Cemetery:** The cemetery is at the intersection of Routes 317 and 6. The grave site is in the northeast section of the cemetery.

MAINE

In honor of Samantha Reed Smith, "America's Littlest Ambassador," this monument stands
beside the Maine State Archives Building in Augusta.

South Coast of Maine

The southern coastal area of Maine is the most populous sector of the state. In summer its natural attractions also make it the most popular area of the state with tourists, particularly sailors. Maine's famous rockbound coast begins right over the New Hampshire border where the two states share a craggy outcrop of historic small islands, the Isles of Shoals.

Appledore Island Cemetery   Isles of Shoals

Celia Thaxter
1835–1894

Poet Celia Thaxter spent most of her childhood on White Island, the smallest of the Isles of Shoals, where her father was the lighthouse keeper. He later moved the family to Appledore, the largest of the islands, where he built a very successful summer hotel. Appledore House, as it was called, soon became the choice location spot of New England writers and artists. It numbered among its guests such luminaries as Nathaniel Hawthorne, Ralph Waldo Emerson, James Russell Lowell, Mark Twain, Harriet Beecher Stowe and Sarah Orne Jewett and one of many artists, Childe Hassam, who produced some of his finest work here.

Through her association with the Boston literati, who influenced and encouraged her own creativity, Thaxter was soon having her work published in the prestigious *Atlantic Monthly.* Her writings about the islands, particularly her poem, "Among the Isles of Shoals," and a prose article, "Island Garden" (recently reissued and illustrated with Hassam's paintings) attracted even more visitors to Appledore.

Celia Thaxter died at Appledore of a cerebral hemorrhage at the age of 59 and was buried on the island hillside cemetery beside her parents. (It is said that her father, Thomas Laighton, was buried "seated on a chair carved from stone, in his rocky tomb, with his face turned toward the sea.")

The popularity of the Isles of Shoals as a summer resort died out after the automobile made mainland resorts more accessible. Hurricanes and fires took their toll, and the island, along with Celia's garden, turned to weeds. Recently, however, since the installation of the Shoals Marine Laboratory, a joint venture of Cornell University and the University of New Hampshire, there has been renewed interest in Celia's garden, which has been revived by garden clubs on the mainland. It is now possible to visit Appledore.

➡ **Directions to Island Cemetery on Appledore:** Viking Cruises (from Market Street, Portsmouth, New Hampshire) makes two trips a day to Star Island from May to October; call 603-431-5500. Special arrangements can be made to be picked up on Star Island and taken to Appledore by contacting the Shoals Marine Laboratory *in advance* at 607-256-3717. You can easily walk to the cemetery from the boat landing.

South Berwick

A little farther north from the islands and inland is the town of South Berwick, the oldest permanent English settlement in Maine (1631). This is where Sarah Orne Jewett, one of the state's best-loved writers, lived, and her home is now open to visitors all summer long.

Portland Street Cemetery
Agamenticus Road

Sarah Orne Jewett
1849–1909

The daughter of a country doctor, Jewett gained most of her knowledge of the countryside and its people by accompanying her father on his daily house calls. She wrote about what she had learned and her stories of small town New England life are written with unusual clarity and sensitivity, plus a touch of humor. Her knack for capturing the regional charm of Maine and its people is most evident in her masterpiece *The Country of the Pointed Firs.*

Shortly after being honored by Bowdoin College with a Litt.D. (the first woman so honored), she was thrown from her carriage and suffered a spinal concussion from which she never fully recovered. Her sense of humor even then was apparent in her writing: "The trouble was that I came down on my head, and there is apparently some far greater offense in *half* breaking one's neck than in breaking it altogether." In March of 1909 she suffered a stroke, followed by a cerebral hemorrhage three months later, and she died in her sixtieth year. She is buried in the family plot in the village cemetery. A large slab stone with the biblical inscription "Until the day break, and the shadows flee away" marks her grave.

➤➤ **Directions to Portland Street Cemetery:** From the center of South Berwick, take Portland Street (Route 4) east to Agamenticus Street, turn right at the statue and the cemetery is $^2/_{10}$ mile on the left; the plot is in the northeast corner.

Portland

Portland is the largest city in Maine as well as the busiest cultural and commercial center. Situated on scenic Casco Bay, its "Old Port" once hummed with the activities of tall ships plying their trade. During the era of commercial sailing vessels, it was one of the country's principal ports for sending goods around the world. Today, the Old Port Exchange on the waterfront has been restored to some of its past charm. Trendy shops now fill the old brick buildings, and cobblestone sidewalks and gaslights lend a Victorian ambiance to the modern, upbeat neighborhood.

Evergreen Cemetery
672 Stevens Avenue

Hugh Chisholm
1847–1912

Evergreen Cemetery is one of the largest in New England, and many illustrious sons and daughters of Maine who have attained national and international prominence are buried here. Many of them gained fame and fortune in the public sector and more than 1,000 monuments stand in their honor. One of the most impressive monuments is that of Hugh Chisholm, founder of International Paper Company—now the world's leading manufacturer of printing and writing paper and packaging materials. At age 13, Chisholm began his career as a newsboy on the Grand Trunk, and by 14, he had formed a partnership with his brother to control the newsboy system on all the northern railroad lines. One successful venture after another led to his founding of several paper companies.

Chisholm's large marble mausoleum is built in the style of a Greek Temple, completely surrounded with Doric columns. A large stained-glass window graces the rear wall.

John Curtis
1800–1869

Curtis began boiling spruce gum in a large black kettle in his wife's kitchen, adding a little sugar and sap from other trees and pouring it onto a slab to cool. He then chopped it into inch squares, dipped the pieces in cornstarch and wrapped each piece in tissue paper. He peddled it locally as "State of Maine Pure Spruce Gum," and it became so popular that it was soon selling across the nation.

Curtis moved from his kitchen to a small manufacturing plant in Portland where his son invented several machines that formed the basis for the gum-making process in chewing gum plants everywhere. He died a wealthy man at the age of 69, and the granite steps leading up to his large square monument is inscribed with the words "Remember the Dead."

Neal Dow
1804–1897

A prominent Maine politician, Neal Dow is considered the father of American Prohibition, having written the Maine law that prohibited the state's sale of alcoholic beverages from 1851 to 1933. Maine's Act for the Suppression of Drinking Houses and Tippling Shops became a national model for similar legislation in other states and foreign countries.

A Quaker by birth and a tanner by trade, Dow devoted most of his life to the temperance movement. He was convinced that drinking kept the poor from becoming self-sufficient. Twice mayor of Portland, member of the state legislature and a successful lobbyist, he was the candidate for the presidency of the United States on the Prohibition party ticket in 1880. He died at his home in Portland (now preserved as a memorial and open to visitors) at 93 after a brief illness, his last words were, "I am very weary. I long to be free."

Jacob S. Winslow
1828–1902

A life-size statue of Winslow stands atop a tall granite pedestal with the famous Winslow flag *W* engraved on one side and an anchor on the other. In 1864 Captain Jacob Winslow had made the blue *W* on a white background known in every deep-water port in the world. The flag was the symbol of the C.S. Winslow company which, in its heyday, controlled the largest fleet of sailing vessels on the Atlantic Coast—if not in the whole Western Hemisphere. His monument is a nostalgic reminder of the days of the great sailing schooners in Maine's maritime history.

➤➤ **Directions to Evergreen Cemetery:** The cemetery is on the north side of Portland, approached from Forest Street (Route 100) to Stevens Avenue. A map showing the location of the grave sites is available at the cemetery office at 672 Stevens Avenue.

Falmouth Foreside Cemetery
9 Waites Landing Road

Falmouth Foreside

Joan Whitney Payson
1903–1975

The small, simple, granite slab that marks the grave of multimillionaire Joan Whitney Payson is indicative of what her friends described as her "lack of ostentation" or "a simple, generous woman with no swank." She was born into a wealthy family—her father, Payne Whitney, was the third highest income tax payer in 1924 (only Henry Ford and John D. Rockefeller paid more). When he died three years later (the same year Joan married Charles Shipmen Payson, a wealthy industrialist from Portland), Whitney left an estate of a quarter of a billion dollars.

She devoted her life to civic causes, giving generously of her time and money to everything from the Museum of Modern Art in New York to several large hospitals and countless smaller charities. Her greatest love, however, was the National League baseball team the New York Mets, which she financed from its beginning. She was a constant and colorful fan at all their games, cheering them on in her blue-and-orange baseball cap.

Her memorial service, held in Manhasset, Long Island, was attended by an unusually large and diverse group of people—ballplayers, horse owners, museum officials, hospital executives, politicians and theater people. They packed the small Episcopal church where her family had worshiped for generations. But her body was brought back to the quiet little Falmouth Foreside Cemetery near Portland, Maine, to be buried in her husband's family plot.

➼ **Directions to Falmouth Foreside Cemetery:** Off Route 88 north; the cemetery is on the right. The grave is near the cemetery office building.

Freeport   *Webster Road Cemetery*
           Webster Road

Leon Leonwood Bean
1872–1967

"Sell good merchandise at a reasonable profit, treat your customers like human beings and they'll always come back for more." Such was the philosophy of Leon Leonwood Bean, better known to millions of satisfied customers as L. L. Bean.

Bean began his enormously successful business by inventing a combination rubber boot with a leather top for hunters. When the first 100 pairs fell apart, he quickly refunded the customers' money. He redesigned the boot, advertised them in a three-page catalog and the rest, as they say, is history.

Little did Bean realize, however, that his store, now greatly enlarged, would become the focal point for the largest shopping center in Maine. On any given day, hundreds of shoppers flock to Freeport (many by tour bus) not only to visit the L.L. Bean store but to shop in the many other smaller outlets that have sprung up along the main street of this once placid town.

Bean, however, rests in peace in a quiet cemetery on the outskirts of town, far from the shopping frenzy. When he died in 1967, tributes to him poured in from around the world. When the popular news broadcasters, Huntley and Brinkley, eulogized him on their program, they received more than 50,000 cards and letters in response.

➤➤ **Directions to Webster Road Cemetery:** From Route 1 north, turn west onto Desert Road and continue for 2 miles to Webster Road. The cemetery is approximately 1 mile down the road on the east side of Webster Road. The large family plot is toward the middle of the cemetery and easy to spot.

The grave site of Maine's most famous retailer, L. L. Bean, at Webster Road Cemetery in Freeport.

Gray   *Gray Cemetery*
Main Street

"The Stranger"
c.1850–1862

This well-marked grave (a sign at the entrance to the cemetery and another on the main path indicate its location) has a poignant story behind it. During the Civil War, the coffin containing the body of a young soldier arrived in Gray. It was thought to be that of a hometown boy, but when the coffin was opened it was discovered that it was the body of a Confederate soldier. It had been shipped to Gray by mistake. Not knowing where to return it, the ladies of Gray took it upon themselves to see that the young man was given a proper burial. Marking his grave is a plain marble tablet with the inscription: "Stranger, A Soldier of the late war died 1862, erected by the ladies of Gray." On Memorial Day it is decorated like other veterans' graves with flowers and a flag.

➤➤ **Directions to Gray Cemetery:** The cemetery is right off the exit from the Maine Turnpike, behind the firehouse, in the center of the village.

Newcastle   *Glidden Cemetery*
River Road

Frances Perkins
1880–1965

Not only was Frances Perkins the first woman to be appointed to a presidential cabinet—serving in her position as secretary of labor for 12 years under Franklin D. Roosevelt—but she is credited with developing the Department of Labor into an enormously effective instrument of government. Her term of office, from 1933 to 1945, covered a period of great national crisis—the nation's most severe depression and its greatest period of labor unrest.

Often the target of criticism and abuse, the small, spry woman served admirably with efficiency and restraint. Laws establishing Social Security, minimum wages, maximum hours and labor's right to organize were greatly extended under her guiding hand. When she died of a stroke at the age of 83, the then secretary of labor, W. Willard Wirtz, said of her, "Every man and woman in America who works at a living wage, under safe conditions, for reasonable hours, or who is protected by unemployment insurance or Social Security is in her debt."

A funeral service, attended by many dignitaries and prominent political figures, was held at the Episcopal Church of the Resurrection on 74th Street in New York City (where Perkins lived at the time of her death). Her body was then brought to Newcastle for a private family burial.

➡ **Directions to Glidden Cemetery:** From Route 1 take the River Road exit to Newcastle, turn right (north) onto River Road and the cemetery is approximately 1 mile down the road on the left.

Thomaston Cemetery **Thomaston**
Erin Street

General Henry Knox
1750–1806

By the time he was a teen, Henry Knox had read every book on artillery that he could get his hands on. When the Revolution began, this made him invaluable to General George Washington, and he quickly rose in the ranks. He was a courageous soldier as well, supervising the difficult task of transporting 59 pieces of artillery from Fort Ticonderoga to Boston (a distance of 300 miles), which resulted in the evacuation of Boston by the British troops.

At the end of the war, Knox was made secretary of war and in this position supervised the plans for establishing West Point. He died at the age of 56, and ac-

The graveside monument of General Henry Knox at Thomaston Cemetery, Thomaston.

General Knox

cording to a letter written by his son, "His death was occasioned by swallowing a chicken bone, which caused a mortification." He was buried with full military honors, and flags on the ships in Thomaston harbor were at half mast. A huge crowd assembled on the lawn of the family mansion, Montpelier, then solemnly followed "a smart procession of uniformed units of the local militia" to the cemetery. An inscription (no longer legible) was carved on his monument: "Tis fate's decree, farewell thy just renown, The hero's honor and the good man's crown."

➥ **Directions to Thomaston Cemetery:** From Main Street (Route 1) turn onto Erin Street; a short distance down the street the cemetery is on the right. Signs point to the grave site on "Avenue 2."

Augusta Area

The Kennebec Valley, encompassing the capital city of Augusta, is an area of lakes, ponds, streams and fertile farmland. Augusta actually straddles the wide, majestic Kennebec River, which played an important part in the city's development. Miles Standish and John Alden from the Plymouth Colony in Massachusetts explored this region by boat as early as 1625.

Augusta

The state capitol building, designed by Charles Bulfinch and made of Hallowell granite, is one of several attractive government buildings in downtown Augusta. But capturing the attention of most visitors to the city these days is a life-size bronze statue of a Maine schoolgirl, which is located in front of the Maine State Archives Building.

Maine State Archives Building
State Capitol
State and Capitol Streets

Samantha Reed Smith
1972–1985

Although this is not actually a grave site (her ashes are in the possession of her family), it is a poignant memorial to Samantha Smith, "America's Littlest Ambassador." Fresh flowers are laid almost every day in front of the life-size bronze statue of this 13-year-old girl, whose mission of peace was known around the world. (See photograph, page 112.)

In 1982, when she was ten, Samantha wrote a letter to the "Soviet Leader at the Kremlin in Moscow" asking him why his country wanted to conquer the United States. The newly elected Yuri Andropov answered Samantha directly, saying that his country did not wish to fight a war against the United States and wanted peace as much as she did. He invited Samantha and her family to visit the Soviet Union to see for herself. She accepted, of course, and was accorded the red-carpet treatment generally reserved for high government officials. Her visit was duly recorded and televised by international networks.

Upon her return to the United States, and after several appearances on national television, Samantha was offered a part in a new television series staring Robert Wagner. She and her father were returning from a trip to England, where she had just finished filming for the series, when their small plane, en route from Boston to Maine, crashed in the woods just $\frac{1}{2}$ mile from the Auburn-Lewiston Airport. All eight passengers, including Samantha and her father, were killed in the crash.

More than a thousand people filled St. Mary's Church in Augusta, and loudspeakers were placed outside for the large overflow crowd (many of them children) during a memorial service in her and her father's honor. Messages of peace were stressed by speakers, from schoolgirls to a Soviet official. The statue, located in front of the state cultural building, depicts Samantha releasing a dove, and at her feet sits a bear cub—symbolizing the Soviet Union as well as Maine. Under Samantha's name on the base of the statue are the words "Maine's Young Ambassador of Goodwill."

➽ **Directions to Samantha Reed Smith's Memorial:** Take Route 95 into the center of Augusta to the capitol building at State and Capitol streets. The memorial is behind the capitol building and in front of the Maine State Archives Building.

Gardiner   *Christ Church Yard*
Church Street

Ellen Henrietta Swallow Richards
1842–1911

"Had I realized on what basis I was taken, I would not have gone," Ellen Swallow was to say later about her acceptance (tuition free) into the Massachusetts Institute of Technology. She made the statement after learning that her tuition had been waived only so that the president "could say I was not a student, should any of the trustees or students [all male] make a fuss about my presence."

She would in time bring great honor to the institute, not only by opening doors for women who followed in her footsteps but by becoming a leader in the fields of public health, sanitation and nutrition and by creating the profession of home economics.

A bronze plaque engraved with her likeness graces the hall of an old chemistry building at MIT. The nose is shiny from the many hands of first-year chemistry students who have rubbed it as a legendary gesture of good luck.

Richards died of heart disease shortly after dictating a speech she was to deliver to mark her alma mater's 50th anniversary. The flags at MIT were flown at half mast in her honor. She was cremated at Forest Hills, near her home in Jamaica Plain, Massachusetts, and her ashes were buried in her husband's family plot in Gardiner, Maine. Her large, square headstone is inscribed with the words "Pioneer Educator: Scientist. An earnest seeker, a tireless worker, a faithful friend and helper of mankind."

In the same family plot is the grave of Laura Elizabeth Howe Richards, author, who collaborated with her sister, Maud Howe Elliott, to write a biography of their mother, Julia Ward Howe. It was the first biography to be awarded a Pulitzer Prize.

➽ **Directions to Christ Church Yard:** From Route 95, take the Gardner Exit to Route 201 and turn right (201). Christ Church is a short distance away on the corner of Church Street and Dresden Avenue and the cemetery is behind the church. The Richards plot is easily identifiable.

Farmington

Fairview Cemetery
Route 2

Chester Greenwood
1858–1937

Just about everyone in Farmington, Maine, knows who Chester Greenwood was. Although he has been dead for more than 50 years, the first day of winter, December 21, is called "Chester Greenwood Day" in Farmington and celebrated with a big parade. Chester was only 15 years old when he came up with an invention dear to the hearts of anyone who has had to brave a Maine winter—ear muffs.

The old adage "Necessity is the mother of invention" certainly applied in Greenwood's case. He loved to ice skate but the freezing temperatures made his ears turn blue. With a piece of wire, two pieces of fur, and a little help from his mother, he put together his first set of ear muffs in 1873. They worked so well that the neighborhood kids were soon flocking to the Greenwood's house, asking Mrs. Greenwood to make them a pair of "Chester's ear protectors."

Greenwood, knowing a good idea when he saw one, improved the "protectors" and took out a patent. He then invented a machine that would turn them out in great numbers, opened his first factory and turned the little town of Farmington into the ear muff center of the world.

A modest tombstone marks the burying place of Chester Greenwood, inventor of ear muffs, in Fairview Cemetery, Farmington.

His factory was still working around the clock turning out Greenwood's Champion Ear Protectors when Chester died in 1937 at the age of 79. Although he was one of the town's most prominent citizens his grave is marked with a very simple granite stone.

Directions to Fairview Cemetery: The cemetery is on the east side of Route 2, just south of the center of Farmington. As you enter the gate, the grave is in the middle of the second row, on the left (it lines up with the white farmhouse on the opposite side of the street).

Riverside Cemetery **Kingfield**
North Main Street

Freelan O. Stanley
1849–1940

Freelan was the identical twin of Francis E. Stanley, and their combined genius produced several inventions. They had patented the first machine for coating dry photographic plates, which provided a fine living for both brothers and their families. In 1898, however, after seeing a demonstration of a steam-driven car, they decided to sell their photographic business to George Eastman, the founder of Kodak. After that, the Stanley brothers formed the Stanley Motor Carriage Company in Newton, Massachusetts.

In 1899, Freelan and his wife made an historic climb of Mount Washington in their "Stanley Steamer," the first car to do so, and the resulting publicity created a boom in business. The brothers manufactured their famous car from 1902 until 1917.

Francis died at the age of 69 in a car accident and was buried in an elaborate grave site in Newton, Massachusetts. Freelan, who lived to be 91, died of natural causes, and his grave is marked with a plain marble headstone. He was buried in the family plot in his home town of Kingfield.

Directions to Riverside Cemetery: Riverside Cemetery is on the east side of North Main Street (going north from the village). It is on a hill, and the Stanley burial plot is about halfway up on the right side. (For Francis Stanley see Newton, Massachusetts.)

Rangeley *Orgonon*
Route 4

Wilhelm Reich
1897–1957

High in the Rangely Mountains, on a site with a fantastic view of surrounding lakes and mountains is the grave site of the eminent psychiatrist, Dr. Wilhelm Reich. Born in Austria, he was for many years a close associate of Dr. Sigmund Freud. Reich came to this country in 1939 and became widely publicized with his "orgone energy" theory.

He developed an "accumulator," a box that resembled a short telephone booth, in which a patient could sit to restore his or her energy. The orgone accumulator was labeled a fraud by the Food and Drug Administration in 1954, and in 1956 Dr. Reich was sent to prison for contempt of court and violation of the Food and Drug Act. He died in his cell at a federal prison in Lewisburg, Pennsylvania, after suffering a heart seizure. His body was returned to Rangeley where his laboratory (now a museum) is located. Visitors may visit this site from July 1 to August 31, on Tuesday through Sunday, 1 to 5 P.M. (also on Sunday, 1 to 5 P.M. in September). Reich's tomb, made of native fieldstone with a bronze bust of him on top, is located on the highest point of this nearly 200-acre estate.

➽ **Directions to Orgonon:** Orgonon is on Dodge Pond Road, off Route 4, about 4 miles from the center of Rangeley. A well-marked path near the ticket office will lead you to the tomb.

Bangor Area

The white pine tree on the official seal of Maine, along with its nickname, "The Pine Tree State," symbolize the important early industry of lumbering that thrived in this area when Maine became a state in 1820.

Wealthy sea captains, boat buidlers and lumber barons are well represented in one of the nation's oldest garden cemeteries here, Mount Hope Cemetery.

Lumbering was one of the colonies' earliest industries, because wood was used for making everything—ships, houses, buildings, streets, sidewalks—and for fuel. By the mid-1800s, Bangor, located on the Penobscot River, had become one of the largest lumber ports in the world. As the western frontier was opened up by the Erie Canal, the lumberjacks and the industry moved with it. There is still much, however, that is reminiscent of Bangor's early trade, including a 31-foot statue of the heroic Paul Bunyon on Main Street. Legend has it that Bunyon was born in Bangor on the day the city was incorporated in 1834, but he too seems to have moved west.

Mount Hope Cemetery
State Street (Route 2)

Joseph Peavey
1838–1918

While *peavy* and *cant dog* are not exactly household words to most of us, in northern New England, they have long been part of every good logger's vocabulary. So prized was this tool called a peavey by early loggers that during an accident on the river, they would often shout, "Never mind the men, save the peavies!"

In 1858 a blacksmith named Joseph Peavey invented the tool—a long wooden pole with a sharp hook on the end (also called a cant dog) that was used to dislodge a log jam. He began making them in his blacksmith shop, and they were snapped up by the loggers as fast as he could produce them. Before he had time to get to the Patent Office, however, another blacksmith beat him to it, so Peavey never fully profited from his own invention. As it was already known as a peavey, his name was to remain forever synonymous with the tool. For many years the Peavey family continued to manufacture the poles and on the family headstone in Mount Hope Cemetery in Bangor is a drawing of this famous tool for loggers.

Hannibal Hamlin
1809–1891

A large, dignified granite tomb marks the grave of one of Maine's most distinguished politicians. He was a lawyer, a Maine legislator, a U.S. representative, a U.S. senator, the governor of Maine and the vice president of the United States. A strong antislavery proponent, he resigned from the Democratic party in 1856 with a stirring speech that won him national recognition. He was quickly endorsed by the Republicans and, in 1860, was nominated for the vice presidency. He served under President Abraham Lincoln as a strong and capable administrator. He later returned to the Senate and in 1881–1882 was minister to Spain.

Hamlin died of a seizure on the evening of July 4, 1891, at his club in Bangor, while playing cards with some friends. Many prominent citizens and politicians attended the funeral. On the day of his funeral all buildings along the line of the procession were draped in black bunting, and businesses were closed for the day. Hamlin's funeral was described by the *New York Times* as "The largest funeral ever witnessed in Maine."

➡ **Directions to Mount Hope Cemetery:** Mount Hope Cemetery is on State Street (Route 2). As you enter the gate by the large Civil War Monument, the Peavey monument is on the right side of Western Avenue (straight ahead) a short distance from the entrance gate. To get to the Hamlin grave site, turn right onto Riverside Avenue. The Hamlin tomb is almost at the end on this street, on the right-hand side.

Public Grounds Cemetery
Mount Hope Avenue

Al Brady
1911–1937

Some 60 or so bullets were fired in less than a minute, but the "Battle of Bangor," as it was called, is still a vivid memory to many people who were living in that city on October 12, 1937. On that day the saga of the notorious "Brady Gang" came to a close with the death of its leader, Al Brady, listed by the FBI as "Public Enemy Number One."

Brady, who had once bragged that he would "make Dillinger look like a piker," was only 26 years old when he died. Between 1934 and that fateful day in October, Al and his gang (all in their twenties) had committed more than 150 robberies, murdered four people, wounded several others and, although apprehended once, made a successful jailbreak. "Never in my experience as director of the FBI have I seen a more wanton display of utter conscienceless criminality," J. Edgar Hoover had said of them. Brady and his partner, Clarence Lee Shaffter, Jr., were killed in the shootout in broad daylight, on Central Street in front of a sporting goods store. Schaffer's body was returned to his home in Indiana, but Brady's remained unclaimed in the morgue. His death certificate listed "bandit" as his occupation, and he was buried in the Public Grounds Cemetery in an unmarked grave.

➠ **Directions to Public Grounds Cemetery:** Drive through Mount Hope Cemetery, exiting the rear gate on Mount Hope Avenue and entering a gate on the opposite side of the street. Go to the end of Woods Road (first road on the east side) and the grave is at the very end (before the fence) in the right front corner.

Old Town

On the northern side of the city is Indian Island, the reservation of the Penobscot Indians. Many of them are employed by the nearby Old Town Canoe Company, makers of fiberglass, canvas and wooden canoes.

Old Town Cemetery
North Fourth Street

Louis F. Sockalexis
1871–1913

There are two well-kept cemeteries on Indian Island, Old Town Cemetery and the Penobscot Indian Reservation, both containing the remains of native American chiefs and other dignitaries of the tribe. Many of the graves are marked by a simple wooden cross, but several large granite headstones proudly bare witness to those who have distinguished themselves in various endeavors.

One such headstone is that of Louis Sockalexis, a native American chief who graduated from Holy Cross College and went on to play outfield for the Cleveland American League baseball team. A bronze plaque on the stone is decorated with two crossed baseball bats and the inscription "In memory of Louis Sockalexis whose athletic achievements while at Holy Cross College and later with the Cleveland Major League Baseball Team, won for him national Fame. Erected by his friends." Louis died of a heart attack in Burlington while on vacation. His brother, Andrew, who was a runner and member of the American team in the fifth Olympic Games in 1912, is buried nearby.

Louis Sockalexis, a native American professional baseball player, is buried beneath this distinguished stone in Old Town Cemetery, Old Town.

➤ **Directions to Old Town Cemetery:** Route 2 runs along the Penobscot River, and Indian Island is approached by a small bridge at North Fourth extension. The cemetery is in the center of the village and the grave sites are easy to locate.

Buck Cemetery
Center Street

Bucksport

Colonel Jonathan Buck
1719–1795

Hardly anyone who has heard the story of "Buck's Curse" can drive through the center of Bucksport for the first time without stopping to look at the grave site of the town's founder, Colonel Jonathan Buck, a stern patriarch who came here from Haverhill, Massachusetts, in 1762.

Behind the wrought-iron gate to the old cemetery near the Verona Bridge, the tall granite monument marking Buck's grave has the distinct outline of a woman's leg on the front of it. Several legends have persisted over the years to explain this curious mark, but the one most favored is that of Buck's Curse (sometimes called the Witch's Curse). The story has it that Buck, before coming to Maine, was called on in his official capacity as a judge to condemn to death a woman accused of being a witch. Just before she was hanged, she placed a curse on Buck.

It wasn't until after he died and the mark on his gravestone appeared that her "curse" became known. Every effort was made to clean and obliterate the outline of the leg, but nothing worked. It kept coming back, and to this day the mysterious leg can still be seen.

➤ **Directions to Buck Cemetery:** Buck Cemetery is in the center of town at one end of the Verona Bridge (Routes 1, 3 and 15). The cemetery is behind a tall wrought-iron fence, kept locked, but the monument is clearly visible.

Brooklin Cemetery
Route 175

E. B. White
1899–1985

E. B. White (he disliked his Christian names, Elwyn Brooks) is considered not only one of the foremost essayists of the 20th century but an outstanding writer of children's fiction as well. Pity the children who have not read, or had read to them, *Charlotte's Web.*

Early in his literary career White went to work for the fledgling *New Yorker* magazine, married his boss (Katharine Angell) and continued his association with the magazine for more than 50 years.

The Whites bought a farm in North Brooklin, Maine, in 1938, and it was here that E. B. began to write his children's novels based on his observations of farm life. He was a prolific writer and continued to write until the onset of Alzheimer's disease, just two years before he died.

The small cemetery where the Whites are buried is at the narrow tip of the Blue Hill peninsula in the little town of Brooklin. Two matching gray slate headstones with only the names and dates on them stand apart from the others at the back of the cemetery under two maple trees—both planted in their honor.

➽ **Directions to Brooklin Cemetery:** Route 175, on the east side of the road going south, in Brooklin. Both grave sites are easy to find at the rear of the cemetery.

The gravestone of essayist and children's story writer E. B. White in Brooklin Cemetery, North Brooklin.

In loving memory of
E. B. WHITE

Samuel Eliot Morison
1887–1976

Samuel Eliot Morison was alternately called "Rear Admiral Morison" and "Professor Morison," which are indicative of the two professions in which he excelled. He was poetically described by Archibald MacLeish as "our Yankee Admiral of the Ocean Sea" and by scholars around the world as "a master narrative historian." He wrote Pulitzer Prize–winning books about such great sailors as Christopher Columbus and John Paul Jones, gathering firsthand knowledge by taking similar expeditions as theirs. His prolific volumes of American history were written in an engaging, easy-to-read style.

Morison continued writing into his eighties, completing a biography of Samuel de Champlain at age 82. He died in Boston at the age of 88 from the effects of a stroke. Although he had lived all his life on Beacon Hill, where a memorial service for him was held at the Church of the Advent, his body was brought to Northeast Harbor. This is where Morison had vacationed each summer and was a place he dearly loved. He is buried in a spot close to the sea. A small stone marking his grave site bears the inscription "Dream dreams then write them / Aye but live them first."

➻ **Directions to Forest Lawn Cemetery:** There isn't a sign at the entrance to the cemetery (off Route 198), but if you're traveling south, it is located just after the Rockefeller Carriage Road Gate House.

NEW HAMPSHIRE

The grave site of Robb Sagendorph ("Mr. New England") at Old Town Cemetery in Dublin.

Southern New Hampshire

The southwestern corner of New Hampshire, the Monadnock Region, is dominated by Mount Monadnock (the single most climbed mountain in North America) and is scattered with quintessential New England villages. In many of these small villages, such as Winchester, Jaffrey and Dublin—to highlight just a few—the local graveyards yield some very interesting surprises. One such small village is that of Winchester where "Mrs. P. F. E." Albee—the very first "Avon Lady," helped to establish one of the largest known distributorship systems in the United States—Avon Products.

Evergreen Cemetery
Winchester Center, Route 10 **Winchester**

Persis Albee
1836–1914

Daniel H. McConnell, Sr., founded his company, the California Perfume Company, in 1903, and although he had a good product, he needed some help with selling it. Fortunately for him, he met "P. F. E. Albee" (women tended to use their initials in those days to disguise their gender), a highly successful shopkeeper and businesswomen. Together they discussed his ideas for selling his product door to door and her ideas on how to go about it, and she was hired on the spot as first general agent for the company.

Armed with her first sample case of perfume, Albee began the door-to-door technique of selling with "unfailing integrity." She was so successful that she was soon hiring other women to help her. The rest is history, as they say, and the California Perfume Company, now known as Avon Products, has facilities not only throughout this country but on five continents as well. Persis Albee is now known as the "Mother of the Company" and Avon's most coveted award for sales achievement, called the "Albee," is awarded each year to the outstanding salesperson in the company.

P. F. E. Albee died at the age of 78, and on her tombstone in the Albee family plot is the inscription "Persis F. Eames, wife of Ellery Albee."

➼ **Directions to Evergreen Cemetery:** The cemetery is in the village of Winchester on Route 10. The Albee plot is near the front of the cemetery along one of the main paths.

Jaffrey

Jaffrey has long been a popular summer retreat for writers, and over the years many of them have made their home here. Ralph Waldo Emerson came here to climb Mount Monadnock and wrote a poem about it called "Monadnoc." Another writer who came for many summers was the great American novelist Willa Cather. Although her stories are mostly centered around the theme of the early settlers on the Nebraska frontier—a place she loved and where she grew up—she chose to be buried in Jaffrey.

Old Burying Ground
Jaffrey Center, Route 124

Willa Cather
1873–1947

Willa Cather spent many summers in Jaffrey staying at a local inn where she was afforded complete privacy and solitude. She was never made to sign the guest register, she used the back entrance and, during the day, she would walk across the street where a small tent, nestled in the piney woods, was set up for her as a writing studio. It was here that she wrote parts of her novel *My Antonia* and her Pulitzer Prize–winning book *One of Ours*. In the latter, her descriptions of troop movements in World War I were gleaned from the diary of a local doctor.

She died of a cerebral hemorrhage at the age of 73 in New York City, where hundreds of people attended her impressive funeral. Her body was then brought to the small cemetery in Jaffrey, but as always, local resi-

A curious cat treads gently over the grave site of author Willa Cather at Old Burying Ground in Jaffrey.

dents respected her wish for privacy, and only a small group of old friends gathered for the simple burial service at the grave site.

Today, however, a well-worn path leads to Willa Cather's plain marker in the far southwest corner of the cemetery on which is written "The truth and charity of her great spirit will live on in the work which is her enduring gift to her country and all its people." At the very bottom is a quote from *My Antonia*—"That is happiness, to be dissolved into something complete and great."

Another interesting grave site in this cemetery is that of Amos Fortune (1710–1801) and his wife, Violate (1729–1802). Amos was aptly named, a remarkably prosperous former slave and tanner who bought his own and his wife's freedom. (The inscriptions on both their stones attest to this.) The Amos Fortune Lectures are held each year in the old meetinghouse, funded by money left to the town by Fortune in his will.

➼ **Directions to Old Burying Ground:** The cemetery is located behind the original meetinghouse on Route 202 about $1\frac{1}{2}$ miles from the center of town. Turn right at the first blinking light, and the meetinghouse will be on your left. The Cather stone is in the southwest corner of the cemetery. Fortune's stone is in the same area.

Dublin Dublin, situated at the base of Mount Monadnock, got its name from a group of Scotch-Irish settlers who were the first to come here in 1753. Today, however, it is very much a "Yankee" town in more ways then one; it is the home of the publishers of *Yankee Magazine* and *The Old Farmers Almanac,* the buildings of which dominate the center of the small village.

Old Town Cemetery
Main Street (Route 101)

Robb Sagendorph
1900–1970

Robb Sagendorph, the founder of *Yankee Magazine* and editor and publisher of the *Old Farmer's Almanac,* was better known as "Abe Weatherwise" to his readers and was often called "Mr. New England" by the local townspeople. Both publications characterize the essence of New England and through Sagendorph's leadership, both became known around the world.

The *Almanac,* the oldest continuously published periodical in the country, is an annual magazine of weather forecasts, filled with wit and humor and has been a fairly reliable source of weather predictions since 1792. Sagendorph said his weather predictions were based in part on studies of weather records dating back to the 16th century. He claimed he was 78.5 percent accurate in his forecasts, against a National Weather Bureau average of 65.5 percent.

Sagendorph died at the age of 69 after a year-long illness and is buried on a high hill overlooking Dublin Lake. The inscription on his tombstone, taken from his own writings, says "Try to determine what the creation holds for you and go with it no matter what." (See photograph, page 136.)

➻ **Directions to Old Town Cemetery:** The cemetery is about 1 mile west of the village, on Route 101. It is on the east side of the road, opposite Lake Dublin and the grave site is on the west side of the cemetery, near the stone wall.

"Ocean Born Mary" Wallace
1720–1814

So much has been written over the years about "Ocean Born Mary" that it is hard to separate fact from fancy. Although Mary Wallace has been dead for well over 150 years, her story is so much a part of New England folklore that anyone in the small town of Henniker can tell you all about her.

There are many versions of the story, but basically the facts are as follows: Mary's life began in July of 1720 aboard the ship called *Wolf,* sailing from Londonderry, Ireland, with a boatload of immigrants intending to settle in Londonderry, New Hampshire. Within hours of Mary's birth aboard the *Wolf,* the boat was captured by a supposedly cold-hearted pirate, Don Pedro. When Don Pedro encountered the mother and newborn baby huddling in their cabin, however, his heart melted. He agreed to spare the lives of everyone on board and set the ship free if the child was given the name of his own mother, Mary. When the parents, James and Elizabeth Wilson, quickly agreed to do so, Don Pedro then presented them with a bolt of green silk to be used for Mary's wedding dress.

In 1742 Mary, whose family had indeed settled in Londonderry, married Thomas Wallace, and her beautiful wedding gown was made from the bolt of green silk. The most romantic version of the story says that years later, when Mary was widowed, Don Pedro retired to nearby Henniker and built himself a lovely mansion. He invited Mary and her four children to come and live with him, which she did, and they had a happy life together. There are many rumors that he buried a treasure somewhere on the property and that when he died his body was buried under the huge kitchen fireplace. (There have actually been digs around the house to try to locate both—without success.) The Ocean Born Mary House still stands in Henniker (now privately owned) and in the Old Cemetery behind the Town

Hall a path and sign lead the way to the grave marker of "Ocean Born Mary."

➤➤ **Directions to Old Cemetery:** The cemetery is in the center of town behind the town hall. About three-quarters of the way back from the entrance gate is a small marker directing the way to the grave site.

Gilmanton   *Smith Meeting House Cemetery*
Route 140

Grace Metalious
1924–1964

The little town of Gilmanton, New Hampshire, was never quite the same after one its residents, Grace Metalious, a 32-year-old housewife and mother, wrote a book called *Peyton Place.* The book, describing the lurid sex life in a small New England town (such as Gilmanton), "shocked the nation," according to the *New York Times.* It was published in 1956, sold 300,000 hardcover copies and more than 8 million in paperback and was on the best-seller list for more than a year. It was made into a movie and a long-running, popular television show; the very name *Peyton Place* took on a meaning of its own.

While it pulled Metalious out of a life of near poverty and catapulted her into fame and fortune, it did not bring her happiness. Her husband's contract as a teacher and principal of the local school was not renewed, she was ostracized by townspeople and she was divorced within two years. Just seven years after the book was published, she died, at the age of 39, of a chronic liver disease caused by alcoholism.

She wrote a deathbed will purposely omitting her three young children. She also stipulated in her will that there be no service and that her body be given to the Dartmouth College Medical School. Her family immediately contested the will and the New Hampshire Supreme Court ruled that the funeral, which her family said "she always wanted," be held. (Dartmouth had refused to accept the body because of family objections.) She was buried in a beautiful old church cemetery, high on a hill, on the outskirts of town. Her grave, marked by a simple white marble tombstone bearing her name, is in the farthest corner of the cemetery, isolated from the others.

➡ **Directions to Smith Meeting House Cemetery:** Smith Meeting House Cemetery is about 7 miles east from the center of Gilmanton on Route 140 (watch for the "Smith Meeting House" sign on the left and drive up the hill). The grave site is in the southwest corner.

Concord

There are many interesting old sites along the historic "Coach and Eagle Trail" in Concord, the capital city of New Hampshire. There is the New Hampshire Statehouse, for instance, built in 1819. It is the oldest state capitol in which a legislature still meets in the original chambers. The "Pierce Manse," is where the 14th president of the United States, Franklin Pierce, once lived. But in recent years a new and much-requested stop has been added to bus tours in this city, and that is the grave site of Concord's own 20th-century hero, Christa McAuliffe, the "Teacher in Space."

Calvary Cemetery
North State Street

Christa McAuliffe
1948–1986

Since 1986, hundreds of people have visited the grave site of Christa McAuliffe, the ordinary schoolteacher, wife and mother of two young children, who became the first civilian chosen to take part in the space program. After months of preparation, with television viewers following her every step of learning the intricacies of space flight, she and six astronauts boarded the space shuttle *Challenger* on January 28, 1986. Millions of people were watching their television sets as, just minutes after take-off, the space shuttle exploded into a ball of white and yellow flames, leaving a long trail of white smoke in its wake. All seven members of space shuttle *Challenger*'s team were killed instantly.

Across the country and around the world, people were stunned by the disaster. There were spontaneous demonstrations of grief and mourning for the victims and their families, and messages of sympathy, including those from world leaders, poured in to NASA. From large cities to small communities, citizens across the nation paid tribute in some way to the victims of the disaster: In Atlanta, although a sunny day, motorists switched on their car headlights; the Olympic torch atop the Memorial Coliseum in Los Angeles was lighted anew; citizens around the state of Illinois left their porch lights on the following night; the floodlights on New York City's Empire State Building were darkened; all along the coast of Florida, some 20,000 people pointed flashlights skyward in tribute to the space victims; vigils and memorial services were held everywhere and at the Vatican in Rome, Pope John Paul II asked an audience of thousands to pray for the American astronauts.

A special memorial service was held for "America's seven heroes" three days later at the Johnson Space Center near Houston where the crew had lived while in training for the mission. President Ronald Reagan spoke before a crowd of more than 6,000 people gathered there (employees of NASA, its contractors, senators, congressmen, family and friends). "We bid you good-

The burial site of schoolteacher Christa McAuliffe, member of the crew of the space shuttle *Challenger,* Calvary Cemetery, Concord.

bye," he said at the conclusion of his speech, "but we will never forget you." Four FT-38 jets, the kind used in training by the astronauts, flew overhead forming an almost perfect V-formation—except for the absent fifth plane—a symbol of the missing *Challenger* crew.

Christa McAuliffe was buried on May 1, at the Calvary Cemetery in Concord. There was a private graveside service with only the family in attendance. A large black granite headstone, bearing the symbol of NASA's Teacher in Space program—a torch pierced by the shuttle ascending toward seven stars—marks her grave site. The inscription, written by her husband, Steven McAuliffe, reads "She helped people. She laughed. She loved and is loved. She appreciated the world's beauty. She was curious and sought to learn who we are and what the universe is about. She relied on her own judgment and moral courage to do right. She cared about the suffering of her fellow man. She tried to protect our spaceship earth. She taught her children to do the same."

➤➤ **Directions to Calvary Cemetery:** From Route 93 (Exit 15W), turn north onto North State Street. Calvary Cemetery is a few miles north of the center of the city (after Blossom Cemetery). Take the third entrance gate (large granite archway), bear right, then take the first left and go all the way to the back of the cemetery; the grave site (large black granite headstone) is on the left.

Old North Cemetery
North State Street

Franklin Pierce
1804–1869

Franklin Pierce became the 14th president of the United States (1853–1857) after a long and distinguished career in his home state. Although born into a wealthy, prosperous and politically astute family (his father was twice governor of the state), his life was marred by personal tragedy. His first child, Franklin, died in infancy and his second child, Frank Robert, died of typhus at age 4. His last child, 11-year-old Bennie, was killed in a train accident just a few months before Pierce's inauguration. His grieving wife, Jane, who called the accident "God's will," did not attend his inaugural and, for the most part, shunned Washington social affairs thereafter. Pierce also saw the tragedy as a sign from God telling him that he had no business being president.

Historians have never rated Pierce very high as a president. Such comments as he was "out of step with his time" and he was "less than a success, not wholly a failure" have been used to describe his presidency. In later years, while he supported the Union during the Civil War, he spoke out harshly against President Lincoln's policies that caused the war to break out. This did not set well with Pierce's friends and neighbors in New England, where the seeds of abolition first took hold, and he spent his remaining years in political obscurity.

At the time of Pierce's death in 1869, President Grant proclaimed a day of national mourning. Flags were flown at half mast and church bells tolled, but his funeral was subdued. His body lay in state at the capitol in New Hampshire for 2 hours on the day of his funeral before being escorted to St. Paul's Episcopal Church. A short service was held at the graveside, attended by friends, neighbors and members of the Bar; all of his close relatives having preceded him in death.

➤➤ **Directions to Old North Cemetery:** The cemetery is on North State Street, not far from the center of town. To the east side of the cemetery is an enclosed area (gate open) where the Piece family graves are located.

Manchester

Manchester is the largest city in New Hampshire and home to about 10 percent of the state's population. It is a city that grew up around a mill that a century ago was the largest producer of cotton cloth in the world, turning out 50 miles of cloth an hour.

While most of Manchester is being revitalized today, its historic past, centering around the life of General John Stark (who has been called the most effective American officer of the Revolutionary War), is kept very much alive.

John Stark State Park
North River Road

General John Stark
1728–1822

General Stark was brought up in a frontier community where he learned early how to do battle. He was a born soldier, and with his knack of being in the right place at the right time, he played an important part in some of the crucial battles of the Revolutionary War—at Bunker Hill, Bennington and Saratoga.

Stark was flamboyant, quarrelsome and outspoken, and his boisterous remarks on the battlefield were often quoted. One of the best known of these was his shout at his troops who were about to engage the British at the Battle of Bennington: "Tonight, the American flag floats from yonder hill or Molly Stark sleeps a widow." Needless to say, they won the battle. His most important victory came in Saratoga where Stark's troops blocked the retreat of General John Burgoyne, thus helping to force Burgoyne's surrender.

When General Stark died in 1822 at the age of 94 (he outlived every patriot general except Lafayette), he was buried with full military honors in a cemetery on his own land. Today it is part of a memorial park where a large striking statue of the general on horseback has been erected.

The Stark family graves are enclosed behind an iron fence, off to one side of the park. About 1/2 mile south of the park, his boyhood home still stands and is open to the public during the summer months.

➻ **Directions to John Stark State Park:** Just north of the center of town (from the eastern end of Amoskeag Bridge) on River Road (left-hand side). Enter the park and turn left at the statue. The enclosed family plot is on the right.

North Hampton

Little River Cemetery
Woodland Road

Ogden Nash
1902–1971

For several decades, Ogden Nash kept Americans laughing. His witty poetry, which broke every rule of rhyme and meter, was probably quoted more than that of any other writer of his generation. Such classics as "Reflections on Ice-Breaking": Candy / is dandy / But liquor / is Quicker" and "There was a young belle of Old Natchez / Whose garments were always in patchez. / When comment arose / On the state of her clothes, / She drawled, When Ah itchez, Ah scratchez!" were repeated by every would-be comedian of the day.

He could dash off a few lines of verse for almost any occasion, often turning bad news into a bon mot. Once, when his car was rifled in Boston, he wrote to the *Boston Globe:* "I'd expected to be robbed in Chicago. / But not in the home of the cod. / So I hope that the Cabots and Lowells / Will mention the matter to God."

Several memorial services were held for the poet-

Poet-humorist Ogden Nash is buried at this site in Little River Cemetery, North Hampton.

humorist when he died unexpectedly of heart failure. One service was held in Baltimore, Maryland, where Nash was born; another in New York City where he had worked for many years and a final one at St. Andrew's By-the-Sea, Rye Beach, New Hampshire, near his summer home. He was buried in the family plot next to the church, and later, his dear friend Clarence Collins was buried next to him, with a matching headstone.

➤➤ **Directions to Little River Cemetery:** From North Hampton center, take Route 111 to the corner of Woodland Road and Atlantic Avenue. The grave is near the stone wall to the rear of the cemetery.

Northern New Hampshire

Heading north along the meandering Connecticut River, which forms New Hampshire's border with Vermont, in what Thornton Wilder called the "provinces north of New York," travelers encounter one of the prettiest sections of New England. Small, neat villages border the east bank of the Connecticut River, and Mount Ascutney, beautiful in all seasons, rises to the west. It is not surprising that many artists have been drawn to this area. The "Cornish Colony," a summer art colony begun here in 1885 by the renowned American sculptor Augustus Saint-Gaudens, brought many of the artistic leaders of the late Gilded Age to this rural community.

Aspet, Saint-Gaudens Estate   **Cornish**
Route 12A

Augustus Saint-Gaudens
1848–1907

Augustus Saint-Gaudens was the most eagerly sought-after sculptor of his day. His enormous public statues grace many major cities throughout the United States.

Some of his best-known works are the *Admiral Farragut Memorial* and *General Sherman Memorial* in New York City, the Boston monument to Colonial Robert Shaw, the *Seated Lincoln* and the *Standing Lincoln* in Chicago, and the *Adams Memorial* in Rock Creek Cemetery, Washington, D.C., which many consider his masterpiece.

After Augustus died in 1907 of cancer, his wife, Augusta (the Saint-Gaudenses had similar first names—he was called "Gus" and she was called "Gussie") began plans to make Aspet a permanent memorial to her husband. He was originally buried in Ascutney Cemetery, but his ashes were later returned to Aspet. On the grounds behind the studio, Augusta had a beautiful small temple made in Vermont marble to become the Saint-Gaudens funeral monument. It is a replica of the stage set designed by Saint-Gaudens's neighbors for a play (the masque *The Gods and the Golden Bowl*) presented in his honor in 1905. Gussie carefully stipulated in her will which members of the family would eventually be entitled to rest here and have their names inscribed on the base of the alter. The Saint-Gaudens Memorial, made up of the artist's home, two studios, picture gallery, and gardens, became a National Historic Site in 1965.

➼ **Directions to Aspet, Saint-Gaudens Estate:** From I-91, take exit 8 to Route 103 east, turn left onto Route 12A north (well marked by signs). A long driveway up a hill takes you to the estate. The Temple (burial ground) is northwest of the main house (map available). Open daily from the last weekend in May through October 31, 8:00 A.M. until dusk. The buildings are open from 8:30 to 4:30 (small admission fee).

Plainfield   *Plainfield Cemetery*
          Route 12A

In nearby Plainfield is the home (private) of Maxfield Parrish (1870–1966) who was one of America's most successful and highest-paid commercial artists in the early 20th century. His father, also an artist, had come to this area to join the Cornish Art Colony at the urging of Saint-Gaudens. When Parrish died on March 30, 1966, at age 95, there was no funeral, as was his wish, and following cremation, his ashes were buried in Plainfield Cemetery.

➤➤ **Directions to Plainfield Cemetery:** Follow Route 12A, $1/4$ mile from the village.

Hanover

Hanover was pretty much a wilderness in 1769 when a Congregationalist minister from Connecticut, Eleazar Wheelock, came here to establish a college to teach both native Americans and Caucasians. Originally housed in a log cabin, Dartmouth has become one of the most prestigious colleges in the country. The town that has grown up around its campus is a thriving community that offers some of the best cultural attractions in northern New Hampshire.

Dartmouth Cemetery
Sanborn Lane

The Dartmouth College cemetery, located just to the west of the handsome and spacious village green, presents a social history of not only the college but the town of Hanover as well. This was, for many years, the community burying ground where college presidents, faculty and students as well as local townspeople were buried. The college motto *vox clamantis in deserto* ("a voice crieth in the wilderness") is poignantly reflected here. Row after row of somber 18th-century stones record the early death of many of the town's young due to consumption.

Buried here are Eleazar Wheelock (1711–1779), the founder and first president of Darthmouth, and his son John Wheelock (1754–1817), the second president of Dartmouth. Other notables include George Bissell (1821–1884), an early pioneer and leading promoter of the petroleum industry in this country, and Laura Bridgman (1829–1889), the first deaf-mute to be successfully taught (by Samuel Gridley Howe).

➤ Directions to Dartmouth Cemetery: Take exit 18 from I-89 to the center of Hanover. From Main Street (by the town green), go west on Sanborn Lane. The cemetery is at the end of the lane (behind Thayer Hall Dining Room), and the Wheelock graves are just inside the gate.

Moultonborough

Traveling across the state from Hanover to Moultonborough and East Sandwich, you enter what's known as the Lakes Region of New Hampshire. There are approximately 273 lakes and ponds in this area, and every town in the region borders at least one. The movie *On Golden Pond* was filmed here and many towns facetiously like to claim "their" lake as the location for it! Hollywood celebrities, along with millions of others have found this area to be the perfect summer vacation spot.

Red Hill Cemetery
Bean Road (off Route 25)

Claude Rains
1889–1967

British-born American actor Claude Rains credited his distinctive voice with winning him his first starring role in the film *The Invisible Man.* Although he failed the screen test, the director said, "I don't care what he looks like, that's the voice I want!" Rains's "resonant, menacing voice" became a trademark and he went on from there to star in 56 films over the next 30 years, prompting one *New York Times* critic to say "It never Rains but it pours."

He also starred in numerous Broadway plays, winning many awards, particularly for the 1951 stage play *Darkness at Noon,* which won six of the year's most coveted awards, including the best-actor citation. Although nominated four times for an Academy Award, he never won one. His performance in the movie *Casablanca* as the wily French police chief, has won him as well as the other actors in the movie, an enormous cult following to this day.

The black polished granite tombstone of actor Claude Rains of *The Invisible Man,* at Red Hill Cemetery, Moultonborough.

When Rains died of an intestinal hemorrhage in the Lakes Region Hospital at 77, he was buried in a small cemetery along an old country road in Moultonborough beside his wife. He and his wife (his sixth) had made their home in Moultonborough for several years, and he was buried beside her. They have matching black polished granite stones. The inscription on his says "All things once / Are things forever, / Soul, once living, / Lives Forever."

➠ **Directions to Red Hill Cemetery:** From Route 25 take Bean Road east (at intersection) and the cemetery is several miles down the road on the east side. The two polished black granite headstones (to the left, toward the middle of the cemetery) are quite distinctive.

East Sandwich *Vittum Cemetery*
Vittum Hill Road

Norbert Weiner
1894–1964

Norbert Weiner is known as the "Father of Automation" and the one who introduced the term *cybernetics* into our language. As a child prodigy he had been subjected to a great deal of publicity due to his genius. It was reported that he knew the alphabet at 18 months, that he could read and write at age 3 and that he mastered arithmetic, algebra and geometry by the time he was 6 years old. Weiner received a bachelor of arts degree from Tufts College at the age of 14, and he had both an M.A. degree and a Ph.D from Harvard by the time he was 19 years old.

Weiner taught mathematics at Massachusetts Institute of Technology for more than 40 years, and during World War II, he made significant contributions to the development of radar, tracking and gun-aiming devices.

He died at 69 in Stockholm, Sweden, where he had gone to deliver a lecture at the Royal Academy. A funeral service was held in his honor in Stockholm as well as a widely attended memorial service at MIT in Cambridge. Dr. Julius A. Stratton, president of the institute, called Weiner "one of the world's greatest mathematicians and one of MIT's most distinguished professors."

His ashes were returned to the place he loved best and where he had summered for most of his life, East Sandwich. He was buried in a small country cemetery on Vittum Hill after a brief memorial service at his nearby summer home.

➳ **Directions to Vittum Cemetery:** Vittum Hill Road is opposite the East Sandwich Chapel on Route 25 (the main road running through East Sandwich). Turn west onto Vittum Hill Road, and the cemetery is on the left-hand side of the road. The tombstone is in the back southwest corner.

Hannes Schneider
1890–1955

Born in Austria near the Tyrolean border, Hannes Schneider, the son of a goatherd, learned to ski almost before he could walk. He actually learned to ski on barrel staves and even won a race on them; the prize was his first pair of real skis. He developed his own method of skiing and was so proficient at the sport that he was hired to teach officers in the Alpine regiments during World War I. He later opened his Arlberg School in St. Anton and taught as many as 3,000 pupils a year (400 a day), including many royal families.

The grave of Hannes Schneider, founder of the Hannes Schneider School (of skiing) is marked by this stone at Our Lady of the Mountains Cemetery in North Conway.

Through several films, most notably *The Ski Chase* (first shown in the United States in 1938), skiing became a great American sport. Shortly after the release of the film, Schneider was arrested by the Nazis for not bowing to the *Anschluss*, and he was exiled to Germany. Ski enthusiasts around the world protested his arrest, and only through intense negotiations was he released.

Schneider came to the United States and settled in North Conway where he opened his famous Hannes Schneider School. He is credited with having done more than anyone to popularize the sport of skiing in this country. When he died, so many tributes poured into the little post office in North Conway, that special help had to be hired to deal with it. His granite tombstone, inscribed in German, reads "Rest in Peace far from your homeland / Until we meet again."

➼ **Directions to Our Lady of the Mountains Cemetery:** Route 16 (Main Street), going north, the cemetery is on the west side of the road. The grave is toward the southwest corner.

Lancaster

The northernmost section of New Hampshire is predominantly covered by the White Mountain National Forest. Many of the villages high in the mountains have changed very little over the years, and Lancaster is such a place. The descendants of an early pioneer to the area, Captain John Weeks, who came here in 1786, have given this little town national prominence.

Summer Street Cemetery
Cemetery Street

Sinclair Weeks
1893–1972

When Sinclair Weeks died in 1972, the local newspaper's large headlines declared, "Lancaster Mourns Its Best Friend." Indeed, the town had lost another member of a family that for several generations had contributed greatly to the well-being of Lancaster. Both John

Wingate Weeks, the father, and Sinclair Weeks, the son, had amazingly similar careers in politics. Both were mayors of Newton, Massachusetts, both were United States senators from Massachusetts and both served on a presidential cabinet (John as secretary of war under presidents Harding and Coolidge, and Sinclair as secretary of commerce under Eisenhower).

John Weeks (1860–1926) was born in Lancaster and later built a summer retreat on Mount Prospect, which is now part of a 430-acre state park. Presidents and other national figures were entertained here. John Weeks was one of the leading conservationist of his day and was responsible for writing the "Weeks Law," the legislation that established the eastern national forests. When he died in 1926, he was buried in Arlington National Cemetery where one of the roads is named in his honor.

Sinclair Weeks, who was born in Newton, Massachusetts, and had summered throughout his life in Lancaster, became active in business affairs following his political career. He later retired to Lancaster and took a keen interest in town affairs. When he died in 1972, businesses in Lancaster were closed during his memorial service, which many well-known national public figures attended. He was buried at a private service at the Summer Street Cemetery.

➤ **Directions to Summer Street Cemetery:** From the center of town, go north on Main Street and turn right onto Depot Street; take the next right onto Cemetery Street; the Weeks family plot is toward the rear surrounded by shrubbery.

VERMONT

John Dewey, leading educator who coined the phrase "learning by doing," is buried beneath this granite tombstone outside the Ira Allen Chapel, University of Vermont, Burlington.

Southern Vermont

Southern Vermont is marked by a mix of the old and the new. Meandering stone walls cut across acres of pastureland that is dotted with red barns and silver silos, attesting to the state's agrarian heritage. Yet the Green Mountains, which predominate here (running more or less vertically through the center of the state), have provided some of the most modern and luxurious ski areas in the East.

Although he wrote so many beautiful poems about New Hampshire, Robert Frost is buried here in Southern Vermont. But he once wrote: "Anything I can say about New Hampshire / Will serve almost as well about Vermont." Bennington, where he is buried, is characteristic of many other small, picture-postcard villages mentioned here, representing the best of the old and the new in southern Vermont.

Bennington

Old Bennington Cemetery
Route 9

Robert Frost
1874–1963

New England's best-loved poet and four-time winner of the Pulitzer Prize, Robert Frost was known and respected throughout the world. When he died in Boston in 1969 of a pulmonary embolism, tributes poured in from around the globe. Many world leaders sent messages of condolence, including one from Premier Khrushchev—calling him "a great poet and a charming man." Previously, while on a visit to the USSR Frost had good-naturedly taunted the people there by reading his celebrated poem "Mending Walls," in which the following line appears: "Before I built a wall I'd ask to know / What I was walling in or walling out" (presumably referring to the Berlin Wall).

His poetry was probably best described at that time of his death by his friend President John Kennedy, who said, "His art and his life summed up the essential qualities of the New England he loved so much; the fresh

The tombstone of world-renowned New England poet Robert Frost at Old Bennington Cemetery, Bennington.

ROBERT LEE FROST
MAR. 26, 1874 — JAN. 29, 1963
'I HAD A LOVER'S QUARREL WITH THE WORLD'

delight in nature, the plainness of speech, the canny wisdom and the deep, underlying insight into the human soul. His death impoverishes us all; but he has bequeathed his nation a body of imperishable verse from which Americans will forever gain joy and understanding." (Frost was the first poet to be asked to take part in a president's inauguration, and he wrote a special poem for the occasion of Kennedy's inauguration).

Memorial services were held at the chapels of both Harvard University and Amherst College, and Frost's body was cremated in Cambridge. His ashes were later buried (after the frozen ground thawed) in a simple, private ceremony in the family plot in the Old Bennington Cemetery. Inscribed on the large slab stone that marks his grave is the epitaph he had written for himself in 1942, "I had a lover's quarrel with the world."

➤➤ **Directions to Old Bennington Cemetery:** The cemetery is located behind the First Church (Congregational) approximately 1 mile west of the town center on Route 9. The Frost family plot, well marked, is on the west side.

Arlington   *St. James Churchyard Cemetery*
Main Street (Route 7)

Dorothy Canfield Fisher
1879–1958

Although born in Kansas, Dorothy Canfield Fisher was descended from two old Vermont families. She spent most of her summers in Arlington, and later when she married a resident of the town, John Fisher, she made it her permanent home.

While working as an administrator at the Horace Mann School in New York, she began to write short stories in her spare time. She was inspired to write by her lifelong friendship with the well-known author Willa Cather.

Always interested in education, Fisher visited the innovative school of Maria Montessori in Italy and began to write about it. Through her books, both fiction and nonfiction, Fisher introduced the Montessori method of early childhood education to the United States. Two of the most popular nonfiction books where *The Bent Twig* and *Understood Betsy*.

She became a member of the first board of selection of the Book-of-the-Month Club, serving as the only woman on the board for 25 years. She is credited with playing an important role in the success of such writers as Pearl Buck, Isak Dinesen and Richard Wright.

Her last major work, *Vermont Traditions: The Biography of an Outlook on Life*, captures the true spirit of this beautiful state.

Dorothy Canfield Fisher died at her home in Arlington, of a stroke, and her husband died six months later. They are buried side by side with plain, matching tombstones in the small cemetery next to Saint James Church, not far from their former home.

➤➤ **Directions to St. James Churchyard Cemetery:** The cemetery is next to St. James Church on Main Street (Route 7) in the center of town. The grave site is to the right, near the stone wall.

Brattleboro

The scenic Molly Stark Trail (named for the courageous wife of General John Stark) links Bennington to Brattleboro across the southern part of the state. Vermont's first settlement, Fort Dummer, was established here in 1724. Today, however, few traces of an historic past remain, as Brattleboro has been transformed into the state's most industrial city.

Meetinghouse Hill Cemetery
Orchard Street

Ely Culbertson
1893–1955

Ely Culbertson had an extraordinary background, but he was best known as the American authority on contract bridge during the early 1930s. He introduced the first successful system of bidding for the new game of contract bridge, and it became an overnight craze both here and abroad. Culbertson not only became an international celebrity but went on to make a fortune by winning many matches and writing several best-sellers on the subject of contract bridge.

Culbertson's early life was filled with mystery and intrigue and reads like a foreign spy novel. Born in Rumania, he grew up in the Caucasus where his American-born father, an oil engineer, had gone to prospect for oil. There Ely married the daughter of a Georgian princess and became embroiled in revolutionary activities. His wife was murdered and he was sent to prison. After his release he continued his revolutionary activities in several different countries and usually ended up in prison again.

Culbertson came to the United States in 1921 and settled in Greenwich Village, New York. He made his living by playing cards. (He wrote that he did this to support his revolutionary activities.) With the introduction of his new bidding system, Culbertson began to enter various competitions, winning most and gaining much publicity.

In later years, Culbertson became a peace advocate and wrote and lectured on world peace. He made his home in Brattleboro, where he died of a lung ailment at 64. A funeral service was held in the All Souls Universalist-Unitarian, and after cremation, he was buried in Meetinghouse Hill Cemetery.

➻ **Directions to Meetinghouse Hill Cemetery:** Take Route 9 west from the center of Brattleboro to Orchard Street (a right turn). The cemetery is on the west side of the road. A small granite headstone marks the

Ely Culbertson grave in the southwest section of the cemetery.

Prospect Hill Cemetery
South Main Street

James Fisk, Jr.
1834–1872

Called "The Improbable Rascal," by one biographer, James Fisk, began his career in the small town of Pownel, just outside of Brattleboro, as a circus tent hand and wagon peddler. His crafty salesmanship soon became legendary, and with the outbreak of the Civil War, Fisk moved to the South where he dabbled illegally in Confederate cotton and bonds. He made a fortune at this (selling the worthless bonds in England), and following the war, he tried his wily skills out on Wall Street. James Fisk teamed up with Jay Gould and together they were instrumental in wresting the Erie Railroad from the control of Cornelius Vanderbilt. Not content with that, the partners made an audacious attempt to corner the gold market, which resulted in the infamous Black Friday scandal.

His flamboyant life-style and reckless ways made Fisk a popular public figure. But his colorful life was brought to a dramatic early conclusion at the age of 37 years. He was shot and killed in broad daylight by a jealous rival for the affections of a local actress. His funeral, according to the *New York Times,* "attracted one of the largest crowds ever assembled together in this city." His body lay in state in the Grand Opera House (which he owned), then a military procession, in full regalia, escorted the coffin to a special railroad car at the station. He was brought back to Brattleboro to be buried; an elaborate monument, in keeping with his sensational young life, was erected here in his honor. On each corner of the enormous marble base sits a partially clothed young maiden, each representing some facet of Fisk's life.

➡ **Directions to Prospect Hill Cemetery:** The cemetery is on the east side of South Main Street (close to the center of town). The Fisk monument, the largest and most distinguishable, is easily located on the east side of the cemetery.

Newfane   *South Waldeboro Road Cemetery*
Wiswill Hill

"Sir Isaac Newton"
1791–1864

Sir Isaac Newton buried in Vermont? This is a question curious visitors to the tiny town of Newfane often ask with great amazement. The local Historical Society of Windham County, which counts many of his descendants in their ranks, will tell you right off—"This is not *the* Sir Isaac Newton; this is *our* Sir Isaac Newton." According to a local historian, the parents of Newton (not at all related to the famous scientist!) were very well educated for their day and possibly admired the achievements of the real Sir Isaac. Hence, they christened their firstborn in his honor. Though not much is known about the local Sir Isaac, his grave site has become a curiosity.

➤➤ **Directions to South Waldeboro Road Cemetery:** The small cemetery is located a few miles from the center of the village. Take the paved road to the west (behind the Windham County Courthouse) and follow it until it becomes a dirt road. The cemetery is farther down on the right-hand side. A tall marble obelisk behind an iron fence marks Sir Isaac Newton's grave.

Bellows Falls   *Immanuel Church Cemetery*
Church Street

Hetty Green
1834–1916

Hetty Green, better known as the "Witch of Wall Street," parlayed a $6 million inheritance into an even greater fortune, becoming the richest woman in America. She began investing in the stock market at a time when Wall Street was run by men only and astounded her male counterparts with her financial acumen. But what surprised them even more were Hetty's odd habits, which gave rise to her reputation as an eccentric. Her appearance on the floor of the exchange nearly every day, attired in a drab black dress and carrying an umbrella earned her the famous nickname. Her frugality bordered on the extreme and was often the subject of gossipy newspaper articles. Stories circulated about her style of living; she lived on the New Jersey side of the Hudson where rents were cheaper than in Manhattan and where she shared a bath with other tenants. Hetty always carried graham crackers or other bits of food in her bag so that she would not have to eat in restaurants, and she sometimes sought free treatment at charity clinics.

Hetty Green died at the age of 81 in New York City, following a series of paralytic strokes. Her body was brought back to Bellows Falls where she was buried beside her husband. At the time of her death, her estate was estimated somewhere in the vicinity of $100 million and was left to her two children. Her home in Bellows Falls is now a bank.

➽ **Directions to Immanuel Church Cemetery:** The cemetery is behind the Immanuel Episcopal Church in downtown Bellows Falls on Church Street. The Green family plot is directly behind the church on the west side of the cemetery.

East Dorset

East Dorset Cemetery
Route 7

William G. Wilson
1895–1971

Throughout the summer a steady stream of visitors make a pilgrimage to the grave site of "Bill W." on a hillside just outside the small village where he was born and raised. Bill W., as he was called throughout most of his life, was the co-founder with Dr. Robert Holbrook Smith of Alcoholics Anonymous. (It is the tradition in AA for members to be known only by their first name and last initial until after their death.)

When he died in 1971, memorial services were held all over the world to honor him. Eulogizing him at the service in the Cathedral Church of St. John the Divine in New York City, where more than 500 people had gathered, the general manager of the group's World Service Office said, "Bill really needs no panegyrics from us, no monuments. We just have to think of the half million recovered alcoholics."

Piled atop his simple white headstone and scattered across his grave are AA "tokens." These tokens, given yearly to members who have abstained from drinking and inscribed with the number of years denoting their abstinence, are left by former alcoholics. One token recently seen was inscribed "35 years." Small family pictures, flowers and other mementos are left at the grave site as well. Bill W.'s home, about 1 mile away, is now an AA meeting place and a guest house for former alcoholics.

➤➤ **Directions to East Dorset Cemetery:** The cemetery is located on the west side of Route 7 not far from the Manchester town line. The grave site is near the top of the hill, toward the east side.

Cuttingsville *Laurel Glen Cemetery*
Route 103

John P. Bowman
1816–1891

The name of John P. Bowman is hardly known today outside of Cuttingsville, Vermont, but in 1881 it was known far and wide. At that time, Bowman built probably one of the most publicized and visited cemetery memorials, certainly in Vermont, if not the country. Upon its completion, he hired a groundskeeper and usher for visitors. One Vermont newspaper reported a few months later, "Ten thousand people have visited the mausoleum this past summer."

Bowman was a very prosperous businessman, but in 1879–1880, when both his wife and only daughter died within months of each other (an infant daughter had died years before), his grief was inconsolable. He hired a New York architect and special designer to build a lasting memorial to his family. The result was the enormous Laurel Glen Mausoleum, which took more than 125 sculptors and craftsmen to build and cost about $75,000 (a tidy sum in 1881).

The granite and marble mausoleum, a miniature Grecian temple, now contains the remains of Bowman himself. At the time it was built, however, his image

The marble statue of a mournful John Bowman leans against the Bowman family's mausoleum in Laurel Glen Cemetery, Plymouth.

was cast in marble as a larger-than-life-size figure, holding his hat, a wreath and a key in his hands and leaning mournfully against the entrance to the tomb. The interior of the mausoleum is handsomely decorated and filled with statuary, urns, furniture and mirrors as well as the four caskets of the deceased. The structure is all in excellent condition as Bowman left detailed instructions and a sizable trust fund for its care.

➽ **Directions to Laurel Glen Cemetery:** Route 103 is the main road running through the center of Cuttingsville. The cemetery is directly across the street from a large Victorian house, the former home of Bowman, which is being considered for a museum.

Plymouth *Notch Cemetery*
Plymouth 100A

Calvin Coolidge
1872–1933

The Plymouth Notch Historic District encompasses the birthplace, boyhood home, and burial site of Calvin Coolidge, the 30th president of the United States. It was here that he received the news of President Harding's death in 1923 and was sworn in as president by his father, a notary public, by the light of a kerosene lamp. Six generations of the Coolidge family were buried in the town cemetery on a hill nearby, and it was his wish that he be buried here also. When he left the White House he said, "We draw our presidents from the people. It is a wholesome thing for them to return to the people. I came from them. I wish to be one of them again."

He died very suddenly at age 60 in his home in Northampton, Massachusetts, of a coronary thrombosis, and condolences poured into the small town from around the world. President Herbert Hoover, who would later attend his funeral, proclaimed 30 days of mourning. Flags throughout the country were lowered to half mast, and at army and navy posts around the

world troops paraded at a given time and 13-gun salutes were fired in his honor.

Coolidge's body lay in state for a little more than an hour in the Edwards Congregational Church on Main Street in Northampton, so that "the rank and file of his fellow-townfolk" could pay their last respects. A simple service, attended by many dignitaries, followed.

A small group of family and close friends, including President Hoover, accompanied the body to Plymouth. All along the 100-mile route, large groups of people gathered to watch the cortege pass. In both small towns and large cities, buildings were draped in mourning and flags flew at half mast. Regular army soldiers, veterans, state and local police, even Boy Scouts—all who had joined in clearing traffic—stood at attention and saluted as the president's body passed. As the cortege entered the rural areas of Vermont, small groups of farmers left their fields to stand by the road and bow their heads.

The weather had turned cold, rainy and bitter as the small group of family and friends stood at the graveside in the old rustic cemetery for another simple ceremony. But across the road, the 400 residents of the tiny village had gathered together in the rain, and sometimes pelting hail, and stood silently throughout the service.

Burial site of President Calvin Coolidge at Notch Cemetery in Plymouth.

The grave site is on a roughly terraced hillside, close to the road, and marked by unpretentious stones. Once asked why he didn't spruce up the family grave site, Coolidge was known to reply, "I don't want my lot to look any better than my neighbors." The only thing that distinguishes Calvin Coolidge's tombstone from that of his neighbors is the Great Seal of the United States that appears above his name.

➤➤ **Directions to Notch Cemetery:** A map is available at the Calvin Coolidge Visitor's Center in Plymouth showing the exact locations of all historic sites. The cemetery is just off Route 100A past the entrance to the visitor's center.

Northern Vermont

The northern part of Vermont is the most rural area in New England, particularly the Northeast Kingdom, where some sections are remote and sparsely populated. In the northwestern section, however, Burlington— Vermont's largest city and only major industrial center—is a bustling community. It is located on the banks of Lake Champlain, not only an historic waterway but one of the most beautiful lakes in America. Ira Allen, one of the famous Allen brothers who played such an important part in the history of the state, founded the University of Vermont here in 1791. One of its most famous graduates, John Dewey, the "Father of Modern Education," was born and educated here.

Burlington *Greenmount Cemetery*
Colchester Avenue

Ethan Allen
1737–1789

When ownership of their land was threatened by the state of New York, the rugged frontiersmen of what was then considered western New Hampshire, banded together into a guerrilla army to protect their rights. Led by Ethan Allen and calling themselves the Green Mountain Boys, they were instrumental in establishing Vermont as an independent state, separate from both New York and New Hampshire.

The Green Mountain Boys were also heroically involved in the Revolutionary War, capturing Fort Ticonderoga and helping to defeat General Burgoyne's army at the Battle of Bennington. Ethan Allen was later captured by the British in an ill-fated attempt on Montreal and spent most of the war as a prisoner. When he returned to Vermont after the war, a hero, he continued his political battle to make Vermont the 14th state in the Union.

Ira Allen (1751–1814), more adept in fighting business matters than in actual combat as his brother was, is best remembered for his battle with the Vermont legislature—which he won in 1789—to establish the University of Vermont. Ironically, at that time he contributed a large sum of money toward the establishment of the university, but in later years, after some misfortunes in business, he was imprisoned for debt. Ira Allen was released by the Vermont legislature, but spent his remaining years in poverty in Philadelphia, where he was buried in an unmarked grave in a Quaker cemetery.

Ethan Allen's grave site is marked by a 42-foot massive granite shaft, surmounted by an 8-foot statue of the hero. Inscribed on each side of the shaft is a tribute to his many achievements, the best known being, "The leader of the Green Mountain Boys in the surprise and capture of Ticonderoga which he demanded in the name of the Great Jehovah and the Continental Congress."

Next to his monument a smaller one is dedicated to Ira Allen with the inscription, "General Ira Allen, the foremost of the founders of the University of Vermont and one of that band of Worthies who, by their exertions, secured the independence of this and the United States."

➤➤ **Directions to Greenmount Cemetery:** Take exit 14 from Route 89 to the University of Vermont (Route 2). Turn east onto Colchester Avenue; the cemetery is a short way down the street. The Allen monuments are in the center of the cemetery.

University of Vermont
Ira Allen Chapel

John Dewey
1859–1952

John Dewey's seminal book *The School and Society* (1899), in which he coined the phrase "learning by doing," created a revolution in modern education. His theory of abolishing rote learning and making education relate to the child's needs rather than vice versa was the foundation for the progressive education movement here and abroad.

Dewey was born and raised in Burlington and attended the University of Vermont. Returning to Burlington following a long and distinguished career in higher education, he was buried on the grounds of the university. In a secluded corner next to the Ira Allen Chapel, a handsome granite tombstone, decorated with the Lamp of Knowledge, marks his grave. The inscription reads, in part: "Ours is the responsibility of conserving, transmitting, rectifying and expanding the heritage of values we have received that those who come after us may receive it more solid and secure, more widely accessible and more generously shared than we have received it." (See photograph, page 158.)

➻ **Directions to the Dewey Grave Site:** The grave site is located on the north side of the Ira Allen Chapel, on the corner of Colchester Avenue.

Stowe   *Trapp Family Lodge*
              Mountain Road

Baroness Maria von Trapp
1905–1987

All winter long, cross-country skiers swoosh past the quiet little cemetery where the Baroness Maria von

Trapp is buried. It is a fitting memorial to the matriarch of the famed von Trapp Family Singers, who was born in Tyrol, Austria.

Millions of people came to know and love the von Trapp Family's story through the Broadway musical *The Sound of Music,* which was later made into an award-winning movie. Based on the first of several books written by Von Trapp, *The Story of the Trapp Family Singers,* it tells of her life as a young novitiate at a Benedictine Convent at Salzburg. She was sent by the Mother Abbess to be a governess to the seven motherless children of Baron Georg Von Trapp. She fell in love with him and eventually they were married.

When Hitler invaded Austria, the Von Trapp family fled across the border and came to America. Maria had taught the children to sing, and when they arrived in this country, without money to support themselves, she organized her family into the Trapp Family Singers. Audiences across the country were immediately captivated by the clear a capella choir, dressed in native costume.

The family eventually settled in the Vermont hills that reminded them so much of their Austrian homeland and built the famous Trapp Family Lodge, now one of the most popular ski resorts in New England.

The snowy grave site of Baroness Maria Von Trapp is on the property of the Trapp Family Lodge, a popular ski resort in Stowe.

On the day of her funeral, cars lined the mountain road leading up to Blessed Sacrament Church where family and friends "mourned her death and celebrated her life." On the altar her favorite Vermont balsam twigs were interwoven with red and white carnations—the colors of her native Austria. One long-stemmed orchid plant rested nearby, a gift from the her close friend, actress Mary Martin, who portrayed Maria in the stage version of *The Sound of Music*. Maria is buried beside her husband, Baron Georg von Trapp, who died in 1947.

➤➤ **Directions to von Trapp Family Grave Site:** From the center of the village of Stowe, go west on Mountain Road to the first fork, bear left, and follow signs to the Trapp Family Lodge. The cemetery, where several other family members are buried as well, is behind the lodge, next to the cross-country ski school.

Greensboro *Lincoln-Noyes Cemetery*
Bayley-Hazen Road

John Gunther
1901–1970

A journalist and author, John Gunther was widely known for his best-selling *Inside* books. The ultimate arm-chair travel guides—*Inside Europe, Inside Russia, Inside Africa* and so forth—were filled with lively, informal reporting that appealed not only to the American public but to the world at large: At least 15 of the books were translated into more than 90 languages.

Aside from this series of books, which had sold more than 3.5 million copies by 1969 and made the author a millionaire, Gunther wrote one small book, *Death Be Not Proud,* that won him great acclaim. It was the story of his only son, Johnny, who died at the age of 17 from a cancerous brain tumor. The profits from the book were donated to children's cancer research.

Gunther died at age 68 in New York City, where he kept a townhouse. He was buried in the tiny hamlet of Greensboro, a haven for writers and artists, where he had summered for many years. His grave site, in a small, rural cemetery, is marked by a plain white square tombstone with just his name and dates.

➤➤ Directions to Lincoln-Noyes Cemetery: From the village, make a half-circle of Caspian Lake around to Campbells Corner, turning onto Bayley-Hazen Road. The cemetery is a short distance down the road on the right-hand side. The distinct white stone is to the right as you enter the cemetery.

Mount Pleasant Cemetery **St. Johnsbury**
Mount Pleasant Street Extension

Thaddeus Fairbanks
1796–1886

Throughout the town of St. Johnsbury, the largest town in northeastern Vermont, the name of Fairbanks appears on many local buildings. Thaddeus Fairbanks, the inventor of the platform scale, came to this area from Massachusetts with his two brothers in 1830, to form the E. & T. Fairbanks & Company. They were soon calling themselves "Scale Maker to the World," and because of their thriving business, St. Johnsbury tripled its population in the next 30 years.

Over the years the family, becoming active in politics, education, religion and science, has endowed the town with its wealth and energy. The town's two most prized cultural centers, The St. Johnsbury Athenaeum and the Fairbanks Museum and Rotary Planetarium, were founded by the Fairbanks family. Thaddeus Fairbanks also founded the St. Johnsbury Academy (where Calvin Coolidge prepared for college) in 1842.

A large part of Mount Pleasant Cemetery is filled with headstones and monuments bearing the name of Fairbanks.

➤➤ Directions to Mount Pleasant Cemetery: Travel east on Main Street, turning left onto Mount Pleasant

Street at the first intersection. Continue to Mount Pleasant Extension, a right turn, and the cemetery will be on the right. The Thaddeus Fairbanks family plot is in a far corner to the right.

Randolph *Randolph Center Cemetery*
Randolph Center

Justin Morgan
1747–1798

The story of Justin Morgan, both the man and his horse of the same name, is among one of Vermont's most treasured legends. Justin was a teacher of singing and penmanship and worked his way to Vermont from Massachusetts in 1789 by his trade. On one of his stops

Tombstone of Justin Morgan, owner of the original Morgan horse, at Randolph Center Cemetery in Randolph.

along the way, so the story goes, he was given a small chestnut-colored two-year-old horse in payment for a debt. He brought it with him to Randolph, Vermont, where he secured a job as town clerk. The little horse, to his and everyone else's surprise, could outrun and outpull any other horse in town. Morgan died just three years later, but his horse lived for another 25 years and sired the "first and oldest of America's light horse breeds." Now designated the Vermont state animal, the Morgan horse is known far and wide for its endurance and docility and as a fine riding horse.

The internationally known Morgan Horse Farm started in the late 1800s by Colonel Joseph Battell, who is credited with preserving and promoting the Morgan horse, is the foremost breeding farm for these horses. It is located in Middlebury (and it is open to visitors for tours), and it is now part of the University of Vermont.

Morgan's rough-cut granite tombstone is inscribed with the words "This man brought to Vermont the colt from which all Morgan Horses are descended."

➥ **Directions to Randolph Center Cemetery:** From Route I-89, take Exit 4 to Randolph Center (1 mile). The cemetery is across the road from the Vermont Technical College and the grave site is in the northwest corner. (Morgan's horse, originally called Figure [1789–1821], is buried a short distance away in Tunbridge; see signs.)

INDEX

Note: Page references in *italic* indicate photographs of memorial monuments.